This book has been compiled by Beryl Holt, assisted
by Members of Berkswich History Society
2014

Cover photograph of Eva & Kathleen Davis
reproduced by
kind permission of
Mrs C. Lockley

ISBN 978-0-9527247-7-3
Copyright Berkswich History Society
Printed by
Russell Press, Nottingham

Contents

Introduction

For well over 90 years the Berkswich War Memorial has stood in its prominent position at the top of Radford Bank. Every day hundreds of vehicles pass it by, most drivers hardly noticing the stone cross surrounded by wreaths of red poppies. Very few have ever stopped to look at the names engraved upon it.

To mark the centenary of the outbreak of the Great War in August 1914, Berkswich History Society has produced this account of the lives and experiences of some of the people who lived in the area during the years 1914 to 1920. Although there were Army Camps on Cannock Chase, the book concentrates on the ordinary people going about their daily tasks. Whilst the war and the soldiers living on the Chase had an impact on the area, other books have recorded in great detail the workings and layout of the Military Camps. This is a book about the Teacher, the Vicar, the Post Mistress, and the other local people who helped create a community.

It is 1920 and the War Memorial is about to be dedicated in the presence of the Bishop of Lichfield. In turn residents of the area will look back from 1920 on their lives and remember some of the young men from Berkswich Parish who gave their lives for their Country.

Next time you walk along Weeping Cross take time to stop and admire this monument to those who lived and died 100 year ago.

Beryl Holt
2014

Part I

Berkswich 1914 – 1920

A Soldier's Lament

I learned to wash in shell-holes and to shave myself in tea,
While the fragment of a mirror did a balance on my knee.
I learned to dodge the whiz-bangs and the flying lumps of lead,
And to keep a foot of earth between the snipers and my head.

I learned to keep my haversack well filled with buckshee food,
To take my army issue and to pinch what else I could.
I learned to cook maconachie with candle-ends and string,
With four-by-two and sardine oil, and any old darn thing.

I learned to use my bayonet according as you please,
For a bread-knife or a chopper, or a prong for toasting cheese,
I learned to gather souvenirs that home I hoped to send,
And hump them round for months and months,
                              and dump them in the end.

I never used to grumble after breakfast in the line
That the eggs were cooked too lightly or the bacon cut too fine.
I never told a sergeant just exactly what I thought,
I never did a pack drill for I never quite got caught.
I never stopped a whiz-band, though I've stopped a lot of mud.
But the one that Fritz sent over with my name on was a dud!

                                        Anon.

Chapter 1
1920

It was already June. Would things be ready in time? Henry John Clay, Joiner, Builder, Wheelwright and Undertaker of Milford had agreed to meet Captain Levett at 9 a.m. Was he early, or was the Captain late? Henry stood gazing through the hazy sunshine towards Stafford. He could just pick out the contours of the Castle on the horizon and, down Radford Bank towards the town, he could see The Trumpet Inn where he had partaken of many a pint of beer after a hard day's work. Now and again a car would pass him as he waited patiently on the rough patch of ground at the junction of the roads leading to Cannock and Lichfield. Most cars he recognised. Dr Elliott, Mr Osborn from Baswich House School, and Mr Smith of Brookfields Departmental Store all gave him a cheery wave as they passed.

Trumpet Inn, Radford Bank

The plot of land on which he stood had been sold to the Parish by Mrs Harriet Turkington as a site for the Parish War

Memorial for the sum of £10, and Henry was due to meet Captain Levett to discuss final details of the work to be carried out before the memorial was erected.

Mrs Turkington had gone up in the world. Daughter of a Beer House Keeper in Lichfield, she had married and run her own public house before being widowed. She was then known as Mrs Swanwick, and became a fishmonger in Salter Street, Stafford. Now she was living in Seisdon Hall, near Wolverhampton, with her second husband William. Did she really need the £10 when so many young people had made such sacrifices?

No doubt she had profited from the war as, in April 1918, she was summoned to appear in Court by the Stafford Food Control Committee. Food was scarce and tightly controlled. Harriet was found guilty of selling a skinned rabbit to a little girl by the name of Lowndes for 2/-. The controlled price for a skinned rabbit was 1/6d, and for the infringement of the Rabbit Prices Order she was fined £20.[1] This appears to be an enormous amount of money for such a discrepancy. Perhaps the magistrates were aware of other such "errors". In her defence, her husband, who had been Mayor of Stafford in 1895 and was owner of Hazelstrine Quarry, claimed that the rabbit in question was wild and therefore the Order did not cover such animals! The Magistrates did not agree with him!

Weeping Cross: what an appropriate place for a War Memorial. Henry wondered about the name and then, in the back of his mind, he remembered stories his grandmother had told him when he was a young child; stories that she had heard from her grandmother about a wooden cross set in the centre of a stone base. Around the base the knees of penitents had worn away the stones, leaving hollows where they knelt to pray.[2] This cross had long since gone, if it had ever existed. He had

---

[1] *Stafford Newsletter 13 April, 1918*
[2] *Transactions of North Staffs. Field Club Vol. LXX11 1937-38*

also heard the story from locals that this is where the gibbet was placed, and errant criminals were left to hang until the crows had picked their bones clean - yet another story about which he would never know the truth. Whatever the history, this was the place where the Parish had decided to erect the memorial to their friends - a place where it would be seen for years to come by those who pass to and from Stafford.

At that moment Captain William Swinnerton Byrd Levett, retired, of Milford Hall and Chairman of the Parish Council, arrived with a sheaf of papers in one hand and a rolled-up plan tucked under his arm. Together, the two men discussed what was to be done - all to be completed for an agreed sum of £54.[3] The triangle of land, in all about seventy-five square yards, was to be cleared of weeds and brambles, concrete foundations were to be laid and a retaining wall in red sandstone was to be built. Stepping stones would lead from the roadway to the steps up to the memorial. Once the memorial was in place, Henry would turf the surrounding

Captain William Swinnerton Byrd Levett (Rtd.)

area and erect a wooden fence to mark the boundary between the memorial and the wooden bungalow that stood close by. The bungalow appeared to have been made out of old railway sleepers and had been built by Sir Thomas Salt as a home for his caretaker-cum-boiler man Joseph Smith and his family.

[3] D 3361/5/89 Staffordshire Record Office

Now, after Sir Thomas' death, the Smiths decided to call their home "Swiss Cottage!"

Captain Levett had sown the seeds of an idea that the Parish should have a memorial as early as August 1917 when he wrote to the editor of the Parish Magazine in the following terms. "It has been in the minds of many parishioners in Berkswich and Brocton that there must be erected someday a lasting memorial to those young men who have given their lives in the cause of freedom in the Great War. Although it is yet too early to decide on the nature of such remembrance, is it not about time that some scheme should be thought out and discussed so that when the inestimable blessing of peace does come we shall not be unprepared? It is the working classes who have given most of our heroes. Is it not for them to say how they would wish their views expressed?"

Not everyone was in favour of the War Memorial. Other suggestions were for a granite cross to be placed on the top of Milford Hills or a peal of bells for Walton Church.[4] Many felt that any lasting monument should be in the form of a Parish Hall or Institute. And no doubt this was a very real need, but it was thought that owing to building materials at present being so expensive this had better wait for the time being.

During 1919 the War Memorial Committee had sent out circulars inviting subscriptions in the hope that sufficient money would be raised to provide a suitable and beautiful memorial. William Morgan, solicitor, acting as the Treasurer, had to gently remind some parishioners that they had not contributed to the fund, but eventually almost £400 was available to enable the project to proceed. Subscriptions had ranged from a very generous £30 from the Dowager Lady Salt, who had lost a son, two of her grandsons and members of her staff, to smaller amounts of five shillings from more humble families and £1 collected from the servants at Milford Hall.

---

[4] *Staffordshire Advertiser, 14th December 1918*

Now in the summer of 1920 it was all systems go. The Cross had been designed by Mr Eden of the Wayside Cross Society, and, after a few minor changes, Robert Bridgeman & Sons of Lichfield had been asked to undertake the work. Everything had to be completed and ready for the end of October.

Once Henry Clay and Captain Levett had agreed what was to be done, Henry set to work. Stone for the wall had to be bought and brought from the Stone Merchants at Quarry Heath, Penkridge, two York stone steps were to be sourced from elsewhere, and he had to order various other bits and pieces including cement, nails, oak posts and chestnut fencing.

Meanwhile Captain Levett and his Committee had to plan for the events of 1st November. The Bishop of Lichfield, Dr J.A. Kempthorne, had accepted the invitation to attend the dedication, and a visit from the Bishop was always an important occasion! The service had to be planned, and Order of Service sheets printed. How many would be needed? Final order – 400. Two cornet players from Stafford Borough Military Band and two Buglers from Lichfield Barracks were asked to attend, and then of course there was a question of providing refreshment for the leading members of the community!

*****

"Thank goodness my boys were too young to fight in the War," Esther Cook confided in Eliza Jane (known as Jenny) Alderson as they walked from Milford towards Weeping Cross. Jenny had never married, so neither of them had any special reason to stand in silence that November day other than to remember their friends and neighbours who had suffered loss.

Mrs Cook's Post Office on the extreme right

The two women, both in their forties, had not known each other for long so as they walked Esther began to tell Jenny about her time in Milford. "I took over Milford Post Office in 1912. We had come to Stafford a few years earlier from Kingswinford, when my husband became the Sanitary Inspector for the Rural District Council. By 1912 my oldest son, Henry, was twelve and my youngest boy, Reg, was seven. Vera our daughter was in the middle and she was a good girl helping around the house so, when the opportunity to take up the little job of postmistress arose, I felt I could cope.

At first it was easy; people would pop in to post a letter, buy a stamp and stay for a chat. There were only a couple of telegrams a year and the letters were delivered by two postmen twice a day. There was only one private letter bag, made of strong leather with a brass lock and key. This belonged to Milford Hall. The Postman would collect the bag from Milford Station in the mornings, deliver it to the Hall and then, in the evening, he had to take the bag enclosing the day's letters from the Hall to the Station and see that it went on its way to Stafford.

Then the War started and everything changed. All men were called up by telegram and these arrived at any time of day or night. They had to be delivered as soon as possible. All the young postmen had been called up and I agreed to become postwoman for Tixall, starting my deliveries at 6.15 a.m. I had to carry letters to as far afield as Upper Hanyards and often did not get home until around 9 a.m., just in time to open the doors of the post office. Our maid did the evening deliveries – I had to employ some help or I would never have been able to cope with everything. It was difficult to find any time for my family, even with assistance.

In 1915, when they started building the railway and Military Camps on the Chase, things got even busier. The camp was built by a London company called Trollope & Colls. I understand that the original Mr Trollope and Mr Colls had been a wallpaper hanger and a painter and decorator respectively, each owning their own company.

Then they became master builders, and at the outbreak of war, long after the deaths of the original owners, the companies joined forces and got involved in civil engineering thinking that it would be more profitable during hostilities.

Every telegram regarding the building work came to my office and had to be delivered until late at night. Some telegrams concerned work at the Rugeley Camp and had to be taken post-haste to Anson Bank. Quite a distance. During this time I brought a couch downstairs beside the fire, so as to be near my ABC instrument, which seldom seemed to stop working. I had very little time to sleep but sometimes I was just too tired to close my eyes.

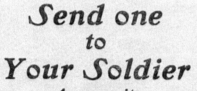
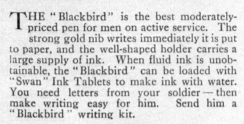
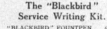

Trollope & Colls employed Irish navvies. They were rough, got drunk regularly, and most could not read or write - but they were very well paid. They earned a lot more than our lads did fighting. Every Friday evening they would queue up outside the post office, waiting to wire some of their wages home to their families. It took three of us three hours to sort them all out, and the bill for their insurance stamps came to £150 each week. This was no longer my little part-time job that fitted round my family! It took over my life. Eventually, in 1916, the Camp had its own Post Office and once again things returned almost to normal. Boys at the Front would write home as often as they could, just to let everyone know they were OK. Each letter came marked "Passed Field Censor".

Sometimes there was just a Field Service Post Card where the soldier had to cross out the inappropriate messages. Mothers never knew where their sons were when they received such a card, but they knew they were alive. I still had to deliver the telegrams bringing bad news to local families."

"My story is a little different" said Jenny. "My family have been in the area for a very long time. My grandmother, Ann Bromley, was born in Milford in 1808 and married my grandfather, Matthew Alderson, in 1829. They had eight children in eleven years.

NOTHING is to be written on this side except the date and signature of the sender. Sentences not required may be erased. If anything else is added the post card will be destroyed.

I am quite well.

I have been admitted into hospital

{ sick | *and am going on well.*

wounded } and hope to be discharged soon

I am being sent down to the base.

I have received your { letter dated_____

telegram „ _____

parcel „ _____

Letter follows at first opportunity.

I have received no letter from you

{ lately.

for a long time.

Signature only.

Date _____ December 31st 916

[Postage must be prepaid on any letter or post card addressed to the sender of this card.]

(93871) Wt. W3497-293 4,500m. 8/16 J. J. K. & Co., Ltd.

Field Service Postcard

Unfortunately my grandfather, a stone mason, died at the age of 40 and the family struggled to survive. Ann had to give up her home on Town Hills, down Stockton Lane, and move to Milford to live with her brother, William, bringing with her the four youngest children, including my father Josiah. At just 14, my father was the only wage earner, working as a Waggoner's Boy. In his spare time he was learning the trade of a shoemaker from his uncle.

My parents were married in 1866 and moved into the cottage where I was born in 1879 and where I still live. The cottage was owned by the Marquis of Anglesey, and then by Lord Lichfield. Until 1893 we had no running water and everything was very basic, just four rooms and a scullery.

Father worked as a shoemaker while mother fought to make ends meet looking after us all. I was the youngest in the family until my older sister Hannah had an illegitimate baby called Agnes in 1894. Poor Hannah died in childbirth and then mother had to take on yet another child.

Jenny Alderson's cottage is on the left.

Eventually, after leaving school, I went into service with the Radcliffe family who lived in Stowe by Chartley. Mr Radcliffe was a wealthy woollen manufacturer. I started as a kitchen maid and then, when I was more experienced I worked at Walton Vicarage for the Vicar, the Rev. Inge and his wife Barbara, as Cook. They were a lovely couple to work for.

In 1912 my mother died and the Reverend Inge retired and left the area, so I returned home to help my father who was now 74. He still did some shoe making and repairing, and between us we ran the little shop from our thatched cottage selling sweets, chocolates and tobacco, just as my family had done in previous generations. I still have an old sign that belonged to my great-grandfather, which reads: "William Bromley, licenced seller of Tea, Coffee, Tobacco and Snuff." Of course you will have seen the sign over my door now. If you remember it says: "Local Picture Post Cards. Miss Alderson Licenced to sell Tobacco."

Once the war started our little shop became very busy. With so many soldiers billeted on the Chase there was always someone wanting a bar of chocolate or an ounce of tobacco. Soldiers would be passing by on their way to or from Milford Station. The Barley Mow and the Soldiers Coffee House, which was on the Brocton Road just opposite Sister Dora's Hospital, also brought people to our little shop. As we sold post cards there was a steady stream of customers wanting to send a message home to wives and sweethearts to say they were safe and back in England, or to say goodbye before they boarded the train for the journey to the Front. I guess they would then come along the road to get a stamp from your Post Office!

Another good seller was the Lucky Black Cat Perfumed Card, which we sold for just one penny to raise funds for Christmas treats for the soldiers on the Cannock Chase Camps. They were very popular with the ladies as they put the cards in their dressing table drawers to make their undies smell nice. They also helped to keep the moths away!

Now everything seems very quiet, all the soldiers have gone, the camps have been demolished and our busy days are Saturday and Sunday when the trains, bicycles and even motor cars, bring visitors to enjoy an afternoon walk on the Chase."

As they reached Weeping Cross, the two women realised that it was time to stop chattering. Quietly they joined the crowd waiting for the service of dedication to begin.

Esther and Jenny nodded to Mary Kidwell who was standing close by. Mary's husband, William, had been School Master at Colwich for many years but when he died in 1908 the family, (they had twelve children,) had to leave the School House. Mary with her three youngest daughters and youngest son, Osmond, came to live in Milford for a while. The older children emigrated to Canada and, as soon as he reached his sixteenth birthday in 1911, Osmond set sail for Montreal to join his brothers and sisters.

Soldiers on Milford Common

Mary did not remain in Milford, and was now living in Stafford but she had come today to mark the death of her youngest son. He had joined the Canadian Infantry in March 1915 and was killed a year later when one of his own mines exploded accidentally in his dugout.[5]

Osmond Kidwell

Two other sons, William and Henry were in the Canadian Army whilst Havelock was a Corporal in the Royal Flying Corps. Another son, Arthur had enlisted in Canada at the outbreak of war, but he met with an accident and drowned before his troop left British Columbia.

---

[5] *Osmond's name is not on the War Memorial but on a plaque in Walton Church and on a Memorial to Rugeley Grammar School Old Boys in St Augustine Church Rugeley.*

Parish of Berkswich.

✠

Dedication

OF THE

War Memorial Cross

AT

Weeping Cross,

✠

All Saints' Day, November 1st 1920,

at 4 o'clock p.m., by the Right Rev.

The Lord Bishop of Lichfield.

It was 4.00 p.m., 1st November, All Saints Day, the day the War Memorial was to be dedicated. Despite the fact that it was Monday, and a typical cold and dreary November day, the majority of the Parish had turned out for this momentous occasion. Twenty-three names had been engraved on the bronze plaques that were now fixed to the memorial; names that everyone knew - husbands, brothers, sons, school friends, and work mates, This Great War was the first time that the names of ordinary soldiers had been recorded for everyone to see and, as the community gathered, all knew that this must be the war to end all wars.

The service was short, starting with the singing of "O Valiant Hearts, Who to Your Glory Came". Then Captain Levett, on behalf of the parishioners, handed over the Cross "In grateful memory of those from the Parish of Berkswich who gave their lives for their country in the Great War". It was accepted by the Vicar, who formally placed it under the care and guardianship of the Parish Council and solemnly charged them in the presence of those gathered, to see that it is for ever preserved.

Berkswich War Memorial

Special prayers were said, followed by the hymn "For All the Saints". The message of the Bishop's address was simple; we should always respect and revere those who died in this war. "They died for Honour, for Right, for Liberty and for Truth". The hazy sun was setting and the temperature dropping sharply as the Last Post sounded, followed by a few minutes of silence.[6]

The Cross was draped with the flag of St George, a gift for the Church from a parishioner, and surrounded by wreaths. In those moments of quietness everyone recalled their lives and experiences of the previous six years. Their lives, and the world had changed.

---

6. *Staffordshire Advertiser, November 1920*

Chapter 2
Dyonèse Rosamund Levett of Milford Hall

My father, William Swinnerton Byrd Levett, had worked extremely hard for this day. It meant so much to him that everything should go smoothly.

Father was the second son of Richard Levett and Elizabeth Mirehouse, and he inherited Milford Hall, his old home, in 1915 when the War had already been raging for a year. He has witnessed, during the past six years, the break up of a way of life, the beginning of the end of all that he has been brought up to revere and live for. His life was devastated in 1917 when his only son, Richard – and my brother - had been killed.

Milford Lodge

Richard, known as Dick, was three years older than I am and he was sent away to school in Kent at the age of five. At this time we were living in Milford Lodge, just opposite Milford Hall. I

Aunts Louisa and Evelyn

was not sent away to school but had a governess, and once I was old enough I was sent to the Hall to learn Italian from my two old aunts, Louisa and Evelyn, but known to everyone as Puss and Mouse, who were fluent in the language. My mother was determined that I should have an excellent education, something she felt she was lacking. Later I had a French governess, and we would walk round and round the lanes forever – very wearisome and dull. I was bored to death and wanted young companions! My closest friend was Cynthia Allsopp of Walton Bury. She was four years older than me and rather old fashioned, but we got on very well most of the time. Almost on the same day as war broke out, Cynthia's father had a mental breakdown. He had been a Captain in the Hussars and was the fifth son of the 1st Baron Hindlip of Hindlip Hall, Worcester. He was travelling home from London with the Ansons of Shugborough when he told them he proposed buying a 1000 pianos! Unfortunately the Ansons put the story around as a great joke.

The poor man had to go into a mental home. This was a complete disaster for poor Cynthia as she was just about to "Come Out". Mrs Allsopp was anxious for her daughter to meet a strong young man, knowledgeable

Cynthia Allsopp

about estate affairs, to become her son-in-law. Unfortunately, the war took many such men to their deaths.

Milford Hall

In 1915 my grandmother died at the age of 93, and at long last we were able to move from the Lodge into Milford Hall, all by donkey cart. It was not far, but when we went over the house it was almost uninhabitable. No lighting, no heating (except coal fires), no baths, one cold tap upstairs. The oven burnt a ton of coal a week and needed to be lit at 6 a.m. The servants rooms were icy, no carpets, hard beds, and rooms all facing north. There was a household of 12 – a cook, kitchen maid, scullery maid, 2 housemaids, 2 ladies maids, a trained nurse, a butler, a hall boy, a laundry maid and a housekeeper. Outside there was a coachman, groom, 3 gardeners and 2 keepers.

When we first came to the Hall, we all thought the kitchen was papered in black. There was no paper! The walls were thick in dirt and the tiled floor was alive at night with cockroaches. Mother soon got rid of them.

My parents suffered great anguish for fear that the War would go on so long that Dick would have to go and fight. He had done very well at Eton and applied to join the King's Royal Rifle Corps, one of the best of infantry regiments. He was accepted, and my parents were overjoyed. He often came home on leave and looked extremely handsome in his uniform.

Our cousin, Jacinth Wilmot-Sitwell, was three years older than Richard but they had been at Eton together for a short while. Our mother and Jacinth's mother were sisters. Jacinth went to Sandhurst in the summer of 1914 and then was commissioned into the Coldstream Guards on 17th February 1915. He was sent to France and in July 1916 we received news of his death. The Battalion diary recorded his death -. "Wilmot-Sitwell very badly wounded and died in the Dressing Station at Essex Farm. Quiet evening until about 11pm when heavy bombardment opened south east of Ypres and lasted two hours, the sky being lit with shells. This turned out to be the Canadians making an unsuccessful attempt to get back a strong point near Hoge."

I was longing to join the war but my parents said it was quite out of the question. I became a land-girl but was not allowed to go to any farm but our own. I was not really wanted; there were plenty of workers and I think they resented me, totally ignorant of farm work, arriving punctually at 6.30 a.m. every morning, struggling to milk a cow that was really dry, and heartily scrubbing out a little barn that was to be kept for a cow to have her calf!

Jacinth Wilmot-Sitwell

In September 1916 I was sent away to school in North London. After the first distressing parting from my mother I was eventually very happy. There were frequent air raids by Zeppelin. None of us was frightened, only beastly! We hung out of the windows in the evening, hoping there would be an air raid. Our dug out was the kitchen, always marvellously clean. One night an extraordinary thing happened. Of course, all the windows were blacked out. While at prep all the black curtains stood out horizontally for several seconds. We heard afterwards that a huge ammunitions dump had been blown up and the blast had reached us.

"Brondesbury", Dyonèse's School

One day at school, a mistress came to me and said I was wanted on the telephone, an unheard of situation. It was Dick, he had phoned to say goodbye, as he was just about to leave for France. Little did I know it at the time but that was the last time I would speak to my brother. He wrote regularly to us[7] and at times things did not seem to be that bad. In January he informed us that he was having food delivered from Fortnum & Mason every week!

---

[7] *Following the death of Richard, his parents published, for their friends and family, some of his letters in a small book entitled "Letters of an English Boy". This was reprinted by Berkswich History Society in 2014*

Fortnum & Mason

FOR THE EXPEDITIONARY FORCE

CANTEEN BOX
For Seven Officers.

7 Dinner Plates	3 Aluminium Saucepans
7 Tea Plates	2 Firestands for use with wood
7 1 Pint Mugs	fire
2 Kitchen Carving Knives	2 Folding Lanterns
2 Kitchen Forks	2 Packets Export Candles
2 Meat Dishes	6 Boxes Safety Matches
7 Dinner Knives	1 Combined Corkscrew and
7 Dinner Forks	Tin Opener
7 Dessert Spoons	2 Glass Cloths
7 Tea Spoons	1 Canvas Bucket
2 Teapots	1 Venesta Case complete with
1 Kettle	hinges, bolt and padlock

Measurement of Box, 20 in. by 13 in. by 12 in.

Gross Weight with contents, 40 lbs. **Price £4 . 12 . 0**

PARCELS POST BOX No. 2

1 Tooth Brush	1 Nail Brush
1 Tube Tooth Paste	1 Housewife
1 Tablet Carbolic Soap	1 Pair Porpoise Boot-laces
1 Sponge	

Packing and Postage included   .   .   **Price £0 . 10 . 6**

PARCELS POST BOX No. 3

2 ½-lb Tins Oxford Sausages	1 Packet Chocolate Rations
2 4-oz Tins Potted Meats	100 Grand Format Cigarettes
(various)	1 Combined Tin Opener
1 ¼-lb. Tin Cheese	and Corkscrew
1 ½-lb Tin Best Dorset Butter	1 1-lb Tin Plum Pudding

Packing and Postage included   .   .   **Price £0 . 15 . 0**

12

Fortnum & Mason

FOR THE EXPEDITIONARY FORCE

PROVISION BOX No. 13

FOR SHIPMENT

For 6 to 8 Officers.

2 1-lb Tins Oxford Sausages
1 1-lb Tin Brawn or Ham or Tongue
1 4-oz Tin Potted Meats
1 Bottle Worcester Sauce
1 2-lb Tin Biscuits (various)
1 Tin (6) Soup Squares (various)
1 1-lb Tin Dorset Butter
1 1-lb Tin Cheese (Cheshire, Cheddar or Gruyère)
1 $\frac{1}{4}$-lb Tin Tea
1 1-lb Tin Ideal Milk
1 1-lb Tin Loaf Sugar
2 $\frac{1}{2}$-lb Cakes Chocolate in tin
Portion each Salt, Pepper and Mustard
1 $\frac{1}{2}$-lb Tin Fine Vanilla Chocolate Powder
1 1-lb Tin Scotch Oatmeal
2 $\frac{1}{4}$-lb Tins Fortnum & Mason's Marmalade
2 $\frac{1}{4}$-lb Tins Fortnum & Mason's Jam

1 Packet Toilet Paper
1 Bottle Figs
1 2-lb Tin Imperial Plums
1 1-lb Tin Finest Carolina Rice
1 1-lb Tin Plum Cake
1 1-lb Tin Soda
1 Plum Pudding
100 Turkish or Virginia Cigarettes
2 $\frac{1}{4}$-lb Tins Smoking Mixture Tobacco
4 Export Candles, extra hard
1 Tin Safety Matches
1 Cake Carbolic Soap
1 Tin Tooth Powder
1 Combined Tin Opener and Corkscrew
1 Pipe
1 Indelible Pencil
1 Box Tooth Picks
1 Tin Dubbin
1 Venesta Case complete with Padlock and Key

Gross Weight of Box 53 lbs.

Price £2 . 10 . 0

10

The Managing Director of Fortnum & Mason, Captain Charles Wyld, wild by name and wild by nature, returned to his regiment the day after war was declared. He dismissed every man in the firm of fighting age and expected them to volunteer to fight for their country. Those not declared fit were allowed to return to their old jobs. Captain Wyld however, was not a man to miss a trick. Fortnum & Mason had agents near The Front supplying mess boxes, and the 1914 Christmas catalogue had pages devoted to hampers to be sent to serving officers. In 1916 they produced an officer's catalogue the size of a pocket book, on linen paper and the first floor of the store in London was devoted to officer's supplies. Anything you could imagine from food (tinned or bottled to stop the rats getting it) to inflatable baths, portable typewriters, guns and ammunition.

It was not all good however. Dick's letter to my parents dated 9th March 1917 asked if they had received "my Boche helmet and fur jacket which I sent home though it is government property. I want to make it into a little hearth rug for your room." His parcel and the letter had arrived in Milford on 15th March, the day after the telegram telling of Richard's death.

Dick was killed on 10th March 1917. My favourite cousin, Joyce Wilmot-Sitwell was chosen to come and tell

The German Helmet

me. As she had lost her brother, Jacinth, it was thought that she would know exactly how I was feeling.

I shall never forget the scene. Outside, in the garden, was a bed of red tulips but the very hard winter had snapped the stalks and they were floating around in puddles of mud. That night I wept so much that I was removed from the dormitory to a small private room. The term wore on; I really dreaded the return to Milford.

Dick in France

Miss Moon, a delightful lady's maid and a family friend, was sent to fetch me at the end of term.

When we arrived at Milford my poor father was sitting silently in his chair. I felt utterly incapable of dealing with the situation, numbed with grief and helplessness. I cannot remember meeting my mother. She was not in the study, but I never saw her cry or break down. I did however cry as I sat and read the letter my brother had left for my parents in the event of his death.

"Tonight is probably the last night I shall be at Milford before going to the front and I am writing this in case I don't come back.

I know how much you will feel it if I go under but don't forget that I shall have died for the best cause a man could have died for and as long as my death has been worthy of a Levett and a Rifleman you must only feel proud and happy.

Thanks to you both my life has been an extraordinary happy one and by a death comparatively young I shall be spared ever having to pass through any unhappiness.

Richard Byrd Levett

After all, if I had lived a longer life what should I have done? What my grandfathers did before me. Lived at Milford, made alterations to the garden and died in the "Red Room", and except to my successors I should have been to the rest of humanity one of the countless millions who live and die without having done anything to make the world better or worse.

Now by my death I have been allowed to do more than that and to pay our share of a great debt.

I particularly want everything to go on at Milford as if I was coming back one day: You know how fond of the place I was and I should hate to think that the old place was suffering through the break in one generation so please do everything as if I was away for a time only, and in every way keep the family traditions going.

That is one of the saddest things in the war, the way so many traditions have lapsed. I don't want any mourning or anything to be disarranged for me.

Do what you like with any of my things. Put one set of uniform in the oak chest and let the R.B.L of the future dress up in it when he wants to. Put any of my letters which you think worth keeping or which might be interesting in the future in the 3rd drawer of the burry which was in Granny's bedroom and is now in your new sitting-room so that they may be with the other old letters and papers which I have collected and put there. I feel sorry that I shan't find them thirty years hence! Your loss of an only son and a successor is very great but carry on and God bless you my dearest parents.

Ever your loving and happy son.
R.B. Levett"

My parents received so many letters of condolence, but one that moved me most was from Humphrey Philips[8]. Humphrey was just a little older than Dick but the Philips family lived close by at Weeping Cross. The boys had been together at Eton and then together again at the Front. Humphrey wrote *"For some time Dick was taken away from the Battalion for a special job and he was delighted when he got back to us again as he was always frightfully keen. He enjoyed life out here and,*

---

[8] *Humphrey survived the war, unlike his older brother Mark. See Chapter 8*

immediately he joined the Battalion he became friends with everyone.

About a fortnight ago we went up to the trenches together to have a look at the part of the line we were going to take over, and talked a lot of the old times and of the shooting at Milford.

I know what a terrible blow it must be to you, but sympathy can be of very little use at present. Dick was killed instantly by a shell during an attack on the 10th. He was buried today (14th March) in the cemetery at Albert. The whole company asked to attend which shows what they thought of Dick. Usually only the one platoon attends the funeral.

I saw Dick the night before the attack and he was very cheerful, and I think he was really looking forward to it. It may perhaps be something to you to know that the attack in which Dick was killed was brilliantly successful and the Battalion did splendidly."

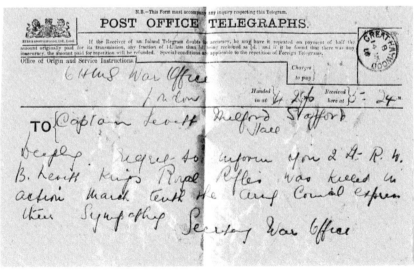

Telegram from "The War Office"

My heartbroken parents had to mark the life and death of their son in some special way and, by November 1917 they had arranged for a tomb in alabaster, bearing Dick's sleeping figure, to be placed in St Georges Chapel in the village church

Memorial to Richard Levett In Walton Church

Last summer[9] mother decided we should visit the battlefields and Dick's grave. It was difficult getting passports but eventually we set out with William Farndon as our guide and escort.

Farndon had been Dick's batman and before the war had served in Egypt. He had been invalided out of the army and was now a London Bus Driver, but he was to be our companion for the duration of our trip.

---

[9] *1919*

On arriving in Albert we found the Cemetery, the military part of the communal cemetery, and, as we were soon to discover, not one of the most beautiful of resting places. Dick's grave was rather overgrown with two little roots of pinks and a tiny rose bush on. From Albert we moved to Aveluy hearing constant explosions of old shells. There was a sea of mud in which the ribs of mules and horses still stuck out. When Farndon was last in Aveluy there was a small village, now there was nothing but a layer of dust. We then turned and walked down the Pozière Road, the scene of Dick's last journey. A cloud of inexpressible grief seemed to fall upon me. The unbelievable immensity of the conflict and sacrifice of youth was totally overwhelming. This cloud of grief hung over me and did not disperse until I had been three days in England.

Now we were all gathered round the new War Memorial, a project that had occupied my father since the end of the War. We were marking the lives of not only his son but of all the other local boys who had lost their lives. And I was now heiress to Milford Hall.

Dyonèse Levett

Chapter 3
Percy Smith of Weeping Cross

The Buglers, in their smart military uniforms, stood to attention on the steps of the War Memorial. I knew all about uniforms from the help I had given my father during the war.

Then I looked down sadly at the names on the Memorial. I could clearly remember the last time I saw Richard Wilton, not so much older than me, but old enough to be called to serve his country. Our parents were neighbours and close friends: his father, Clerk to the Stafford Board of Guardians, was the Vicar's Warden and mine was a Church Warden at Baswich Church.

I was cycling back to King Edward VIth Grammar School one afternoon, and was wearing my gear for a Cadet Corps meeting. I was running late. Richard was walking the other way in the uniform of a Second Lieutenant in the 9th Yorkshire Regiment. He called out a greeting and waved but I did not have time to stop. That was the last time I would see him. When next I met his mother she said that he had told her to advise me that I should keep out of the Cadet Corps, as he knew what it would lead to. It was shortly after this that the tragic news of his death arrived. Richard had been killed in action south of Polygon Wood while gallantly defending a post of which he was in command. He was only twenty-one and his body has never been found.[10] Richard went to France for the first time in April 1915, at the age of 19, within a month he was "gassed" and returned home to recuperate. In the November, after receiving his commission, he returned to France and had gone through all the fighting on the Somme in July 1916. Although they had lost a much-loved son, the family were justly

---

[10] *Richard is recorded on the Tyne Cot Memorial which bears the names of almost 35,000 officers and men whose graves are not known. The memorial, designed by Sir Herbert Baker with sculpture by Joseph Armitage and F.V. Blundstone, was unveiled by Sir Gilbert Dyett on 20 June 1927.*

　　　　　　　　(c) Berkswich History Society

proud of the letter sent from his colonel, who wrote, "Your son's Company was a part of the line against which the Germans launched a desperate counter attack, and it was due to their gallantry and devotion to duty that the enemy did not gain a footing. There were four officers in the company, all of whom died gallantly at their posts sooner than be driven back and their names will be forever remembered by the Yorkshire Regiment."

Richard's parents, sister Dorothy and younger brother Clifford.

Another pupil from the Grammar School whose name is on the War Memorial is Alan Frederick Green. The family live on Radford Bank, only a few yards away from the memorial. Alan was a similar age to Richard Wilton but I can only just remember him as he went off to New Zealand in September 1913 to farm. He was not away long for, in 1916, he joined the 2nd Battalion of the New Zealand Rifle Brigade and they set sail from Wellington for Plymouth on 11th October 1916. They were soon involved in fighting in France and Belgium. Alan was killed in action during the Battle of Messines on 7th June 1917.[11]

I live with my parents in a house called "Inglestone" at Weeping Cross. There were only a few houses along this stretch of road at the outbreak of War, but there were children in almost all of them and we spent many happy hours roaming the fields around the area. In 1914 my father was the joint owner of "Brookfields", Gents, Ladies and Boys outfitters.

A tragic accident in the Brookfield family had given my father the opportunity to buy into the business. The Brookfield brothers were eminent business men in Stafford, were bachelors, and lived in some style at Thornhurst,[12] Rowley Bank. They regularly rode up onto Cannock Chase.

In December 1909 father was returning from Church with Mr Wilton from "Hillcrest" when they saw, at the top of Baswich Lane, horses, riders and other people standing round in a group. As they drew nearer they could see the figure of Mr Stuart Brookfield lying on the ground. He had been thrown from his horse against the wall of Baswich House grounds and had been killed instantly. Arthur Brookfield was devastated. He had lost his brother, and his business partner, and so it was that he encouraged my father to develop the new business in premises close to the Ancient High House.

The new Brookfields' consisted of a Gents' department on the ground floor and a Boys and Ladies' Department on the first floor. As an apprentice father had been trained to measure

---

[11] *The Messines Ridge (New Zealand) Memorial stands within Messines Ridge British Cemetery and commemorates over 800 soldiers of the New Zealand Expeditionary Force who died in or near Messines in 1917 and 1918 and who have no known grave. This is one of seven memorials in France and Belgium to those New Zealand soldiers who died on the Western Front and whose graves are not known. The memorials are all in cemeteries chosen as appropriate to the fighting in which the men died.*
[12] *Now Abbeyfield.*

ladies as well as men for their garments. The original Ladies Department had been only a measuring costumiers, but now there was a Ladies Tailoring Room with skilled tailoresses, and everything could be made on the premises including model gowns, for which the shop had an excellent reputation.

When the War arrived, Brookfields' shop became extremely busy supplying uniforms to the officers who were posted to the two, ever-growing transit camps on Cannock Chase. Brookfields established a shop in one half of one of the huts at Brocton Camp. It was in Row "H". Father appointed Mr Borland, a retired Wolverhampton tailor, to run it for him. The firm provided Mr Borland with a Humber car, purchased second hand from Mr Mead of Gaol Square Garage. It had a winding handle and no battery!

Mr Borland measured officers for their uniforms and took their orders. The officers would only have a few days' notice of their posting, so time was at a premium. The orders were delivered to Brookfields' main shop that afternoon and telephoned to either Morton & Joint or John Barron, two firms in Leeds. After school on Saturdays (we went to school

The "new" Brookfields

on Saturday morning but had Wednesday afternoon free) and in the school holidays, I had to go to work at the shop. I entered the camp orders in a special ledger and took the emergency deliveries to the camp shop on my bicycle. I worked all hours! Mother complained repeatedly, but father was merciless and paid me a pittance for all the hours I put in.

TO

PARENTS & GUARDIANS

We wish to draw your attention to our Showroom of **Boys' Clothing** and **Outfitting.**

Tunic Suits.
School Suits.
Overcoats.
Raincoats.
Jerseys.
Knickers.
Shirts.
Underwear.
etc., etc.

Complete School Outfits a Special Feature.

BROOKFIELDS, 51 & 52, Greengate St., STAFFORD.

Brookfields Advertisement from 1917

The completed goods would arrive at Stafford Station within forty-eight hours and were transported to the camp by whatever means available – military vehicle, Mr Borland's Humber or the bicycle basket of my bike. A boy doing a man's job from the age of eleven! Ordinary ranks had regulation supply uniforms and ill-fitting they were!

The Leeds tailoring firms employed many Jewish people who were prepared to work all hours to ensure that the orders were completed on time. Such firms were common throughout the industrial areas of Lancashire and Yorkshire. They prospered, together with spinning and weaving companies. In other parts of the country tanners, boot makers, hosiers, hatters, button and buckle-makers, ribbon and badge makers, glovers and saddlers, also prospered – businesses like ours went from strength to strength. Stafford's boot making industry also flourished.

During the War Brookfields' employed extra women just to sew on badges. Some men progressed so quickly - each time they were promoted all the significant badge changes had to be made. Brookfields' also supplied the swagger sticks which Regimental Sergeant Major's carried. Made of twisted willow, they had decorative leather bound handles fixed with a brass screw finial.

Cecil Mehlort was in my class at school. His father, a German citizen, and brother worked at Siemens' as engineers. When War was declared many German families departed very swiftly for their homeland. Our friends the Grotefeldts who lived just a few doors away, nearer to Baswich Lane, did not leave, but they were subject to a kind of internment. They had to move to a house within one mile of the centre of Stafford and report regularly to the Police Station. Father forbade my brother Sid, from playing with his friends, the Grotefeldts, once the war had started. Sid was headstrong and regularly climbed out of his bedroom window to go and join his German mates even though it meant the slipper if father found out. The Mehlorts remained in their home as they were nearer the town centre and Mrs Mehlort was English! Herr Schaeffer, the Managing Director of Siemens' did leave, and our neighbour Mr Parker took over. This exodus of German workers made it considerably easier for the management to turn production over to war work.

The father of a boy at school was the manager of a little cinema in Tipping Street called "The Picture Palace". On Friday afternoons he would give his son a few tickets to sell to his school friends for the Saturday morning showing of silent films

The Picture House, Stafford

such as Charlie Chaplin. The lucky ones would turn up next morning, with a few hopefuls hanging on. If the manager was in a good mood he might let us in for free. Then on 23rd February, 1914 the brand new "Picture House " opened and this was the beginning of the end for the Picture Palace. I greatly missed these Saturday morning trips to the cinema when father insisted that I went to help in the shop.

The trainee soldiers on Cannock Chase had to march from Brocton, down Cannock Road, round Weeping Cross, along the Lichfield Road to Milford, back to Brocton and then up the hill to the Camp. They carried weapons and 56lb packs on their backs. A band would march with them to help them keep time. The fitter soldiers would sing as they marched such songs as "Tipperary" and "Goodbye Dolly Grey". The poor men, many of them hardly more than boys, had ill-fitting boots that caused them terrible blisters. Some of them would collapse with discomfort and fatigue and it was a common occurrence for a soldier to knock on a door with a request from an officer in charge, for water to be brought out. Most local children would rush out to watch when we heard the band coming. Often at weekends the band would give a concert at the Borough Hall. There was no charge to attend but a collection box was passed round.

YOUR COUNTRY NEEDS YOU

I started at King Edward VIth Grammar School in September 1915, when I was twelve and a half. Because of the War, the staff was cut to a skeleton: those teachers who were too old or unfit to be called-up had to teach more subjects than before, retired teachers were brought in, and anyone else with an academic or practical bent was called upon. More men were sent to fight. Eventually we even had lady teachers!

As the War continued we all carried on with our out-of-school jobs, working longer and longer hours. It was exhausting, but we could not avoid seeing the posters- "Your Country Needs You" and it seemed to us all that Kitchener was pointing at us, not just to those of our senior schoolfellows who had turned seventeen. The King[13] had also made an appeal: "I ask you, men of all classes, to come forward voluntarily and take your share of the fight"

---

[13] George V

Will Greatrex lived very near to the school. His father kept The Grapes Hotel, and he had taken over the Motor House adjacent to the Hotel, in Newport Road, from Lea & Son who had started it in 1910. Mr Greatrex ran a taxi service from the premises and empty petrol cans could be exchanged there for a full one. There were, as yet, no petrol pumps for public use.

Will Greatrex with his Taxi.

Will had perhaps the most responsible out of school job of all my classmates. He had learned to drive his father's taxis and he drove soldiers between Stafford station and the camps at Brocton and Rugeley Bank. This substantially increased his family's income as well as providing a valuable service. However, Will was below the statutory age of 17 to be in charge of a vehicle and was repeatedly brought up before the Stafford magistrates. But his father encouraged him to continue the taxi-ing. It was, he told his customers, cheaper to pay Will's fines than to do without the business!!!

Sidney Venables, who was two standards above me at school, had to leave to help run the family timber merchants business at Doxey. The timber yard had become a storage depot for sawn wood from mills all over the country. The yard was very busy, with railway wagons always waiting to be unloaded. Manpower was in short supply so trusted German prisoners of war came from Brocton Camp each day by train from Milford to help. They were of course always under armed guard as there would be a great temptation to escape while working so close to the railway station. It would have been easy to slip away.

For my fourteenth birthday I was given a camera and I began by taking photographs of our house, the family and the pet rabbits. Much to my surprise, in the school holidays before my fifteenth birthday my father asked his friends the Eymer brothers, who ran a photographic service from their chemist shop in Greengate Street, if they would allow me to go on Wednesday afternoons and learn how to develop and print my own films. I eventually set up my own "dark room" in a large cupboard in my bedroom. I draped black fabric over the cracks around the door and locked myself in so that my younger brothers could not disturb me. I wondered afterwards how it was that I did not asphyxiate myself.

I was able to photograph a bi-plane that came down in the field behind our house. The Royal Flying Corps pilot was unhurt, but within minutes it seemed that every small boy within a radius of five miles had arrived to inspect the plane. There was quite a crowd, and when it eventually took off again people's hats went flying in all directions!

When I was fourteen, I joined the School Cadet Corps. Most pupils belonged, as with increasing reports of casualties at the Front, we felt it our duty to be acquainted with war weapons and techniques, however fearsome. Our families encouraged this. The School Cadet Corps was attached to the 6th North

My Photograph

Staffordshire Regiment. Captain Kidder was our instructor. We wore khaki uniform – breeches, puttees, tunic, flat-topped caps, long khaki socks and army boots. We had drill several times a week but as every rifle was needed in France, we had wooden ones for drill purposes! On Saturday and Wednesday afternoons we went on route marches of at least four miles. These marches often included mock battles at Stafford Castle or Hopton Heath. We carried packs of 28lbs and, of course, our dummy rifles.

One day we were marching down Weston Bank when an old man came out with a basket of eating apples for us. We broke rank. Captain Kidder was furious and gave everyone a good dressing down. Part of our training took place at Brocton Camp. We had to march, four abreast, to the camp. Captain Jennion was the Bombing Instructor to the troops and he also instructed us. There were mock trenches to ensure that the basic training was undertaken in conditions as near as possible to reality.

We were taught how to throw bombs! These were of two types. One was a hand-held grenade, from which you had to withdraw the pin, and then throw it before three minutes had elapsed. After that it went off! The other was one that you placed in a trench catapult. The grenade, which had no pin was placed on a platform, the lever pulled down to compress a spring, then released to fire it. If it was fired correctly, it travelled much further than a thrown grenade.

King Edward VIth Grammar School

Every six months, the Army Recruiting Officer from the Drill Hall opposite our school came round. He was a retired Regimental Sergeant Major. He carried lists of pupil's names on a clip-board under his arm and a pencil in his top pocket. The Cadet Corps paraded in front of him and those who were due to leave school within the next six months were reviewed. He singled out the ones he felt could go straight into the Forces and wrote something against their names on his list.

When they were seventeen-and-a-half those listed received notification to go for an appointment with a Health Inspector at a Regimental Centre. If they did not pass they were not called up. If they did pass they were soon sent an official letter to tell them when and where to report. Boys who

Percy Smith

wished to enter the Flying Corps had to have a special test. They were spun in a revolving chair. If they could get up and walk in a straight line immediately, they were accepted!

During the last summer of the War a young soldier, called Eddie Dunhill, came from Brocton Camp to help at Baswich Farm. There was an official scheme whereby a number of recruits who came from rural areas could do some of their War Service on farms. Eddie came from somewhere in the South-West and he taught me many things about country ways. I bought a .410 single-barrel shotgun and the pair of us went rabbiting in the long, summer evenings. We would take a decoy rabbit: a rabbit pelt stuffed with wood-shavings, so that it would stand up. It would be placed near the entrance to a large burrow, and then we would wait. Eventually six or seven rabbits would decide that it was safe to come out. They were an easy target and a useful supplement to our diet. You did not have to have a licence to own a gun, and cartridges were readily available. When there was no-one about we would sometimes escape to the garden shed. We would clap a cartridge into the vice, which was attached to the work bench, and then standing well back, with arm extended, hit the cartridge with a hammer!

You could leave King Edward's at any time, but your parents were meant to give a term's notice. If they didn't, the three guineas for the term had to be paid. Then, in 1918, during an English lesson which Mr Powell, the headmaster, was taking, the classroom door opened and Joseph Park came in with a note which he handed to the headmaster, who read it and then call me out. He said that my father needed me at the shop. When I got there, father told me to take off my coat and start serving the customers. He said that I would never be going back to school. I was fourteen and a half. My pay to start was the same as it had been when I had worked in the school holidays - ten shillings a week. When I was fifteen, Mother complained to Father and he increased my wages to twelve and sixpence a week. I had to work a twelve-hour day, sometimes longer, and a seven day week.

As a small boy I learned to recognise the customers. I watched how the assistants behaved and studied how to make polite conversation. I had been shown how to open doors for ladies and carry their parcels to their waiting vehicles. As I grew up I naturally became interested in people, perceptive to their needs, and derived satisfaction from helping them. This now, was to be my way of life for the foreseeable future.

Chapter 4
Laura Dutton of Walton Village

Laura Dutton

When war was declared on Germany on 4th August 1914, I was not quite 12 and still at school. Now I am approaching my 18th birthday and have been working for Mr Hourd at the Stafford Newsletter for almost four years. I turned to look out of the corner of my eye at the slight figure of our neighbour, Jemima Trundley, who stood between my mother and me. Tears were trickling down the face of the old lady who had lost her son, Jim, in Belgium during September 1917. His body had never been found after fierce fighting in an attempt to capture Passchendaele[14]

Mrs Trundley was usually a bright and happy person and, when she received news that Jim was missing, she never gave up hope that he would be safe, although she had confided in my mother that she thought he was dead. But it was not to be. Eventually the fateful letter arrived to say that Jim was dead. The sight of his name on the War Memorial was just too much for Mrs Trundley who was now alone in the world. Her husband had died in 1907 and Jim was her only child. As she stood by the Memorial she gave thanks for the kind neighbours and friends who had helped and supported her since Jim had enlisted.

---

[14] *James Trundley's name is recorded on the Tyne Cot Memorial, one of four memorials to the missing in Belgian Flanders, which cover the area known as the Ypres Salient.*

Trundley's had been our neighbours for almost the whole of my life and, over the years, I spent many happy hours in the company of Jemima Trundley and Jim. It was only when Jim was conscripted into the North Staffordshire Regiment that I realise just what it all meant. The call went out for recruits between the ages of nineteen and thirty. As my father William was forty-three, he was able to remain at home and continue working as a bricklayer. It was a great relief to mother and I.

One day an envelope arrived addressed to Jim. When he opened it he found a white feather inside. White feathers, a symbol of cowardice, were distributed by women of the Order of the White Feather to any man they saw who was not in uniform and seemed capable of joining the army. Jim was no coward; he was at home helping to produce the food we all needed.

Although he had no wish to leave his mother alone, for Jim, single and now twenty-eight, joining up was a chance for travel and excitement. He had been working for Mr Joseph Burton of Congreve House, Walton, as a general labourer for a number of years; sometimes he helped with the farm and sometimes with the odd bit of building work. His journey from home to work each morning was less than a hundred yards. Even before they came to Walton the family lived in a cottage on the farm where he worked. He had never been far from home. Now he could look forward to adventure and seeing more of the world.

Laura's Parents

As the war progressed things gradually got worse. Fabric for dressmaking was of very poor quality and expensive. Most parents had to unpick garments and remake them to fit the next child in the family and very rarely did mum get anything new. The Manchester and Bradford Warehouse in Greengate Street, Stafford, opposite Tipping Street, ran a clothing club in several villages. There was one in Walton. When your card showed thirty shillings they added on an extra shilling! Money was saved mostly for children's clothes, perhaps a winter coat or dress.

Food became scarce and every-one was urged to grow as many vegetables as possible. Most houses in the village had large gardens and the men, and some wives, spent most of their spare time in the fresh air planting carrots, potatoes and turnips to put into earth clamps providing frost-free storage so that there were root vegetables in the winter.

There was always plenty of fruit growing on the trees, apples, pears, plums, and in the autumn we all went blackberrying. Mother was a great cook. She had met my father while working as cook to Mr Fairhurst, a barrister, who lived at the big house in the village, and she was always busy making bread, pies, jam and such like.

Laura & Mrs Trundley

Of course, poor Mrs Trundley had no-one to do her garden, although my father tried to help where he could. As time passed, trusted Prisoners of War from Brocton Camp were allowed out under guard, to help those whose husbands and sons had been called up. One day four German boys escorted by a British soldier arrived to dig her garden. I don't know how many cups of tea she made that day although a neighbour criticised her for providing comfort for the Germans. This upset her greatly as she knew that the lads had no more desire to fight than her own son. These Prisoners of War never made any attempt to escape. They knew that they were being relatively well treated and should they manage to escape and get back over the Channel they would be expected to fight again. Something they had no wish to do.

Jacob's Ladder

Early in 1915 we began to see changes in the Parish. There were already one hundred soldiers billeted in Milford and there were rumours that 20,000 would come to camp on the Chase before long[15]

My favourite walk was to go to Jacob's Ladder with my school friends. We would take off our shoes and socks and sit with our feet dangling in the stream before climbing up Jacob's ladder, trying to climb the old oak tree, without success, and then racing back up the hill for tea. But one day, on a sunny Spring Sunday we were tempted to go further afield. We had heard that they had started building a new road across the Chase from the Green at Brocton, over Anson Bank and back to Brocton Gate Farm. The carpenters who were going to build the huts had also started to arrive. We just had to go and look. One Sunday there was nothing, by the following Sunday there were thirty huts and after that there were huts all over the Chase.

[15] *Berkswich Parish Magazine February 1915.*

**Built for Swansea Docks and sold circa 1915 to Cannock &
Rugeley Colliery Co to work on Cannock Chase**

A new railway was also built to get supplies up to Brocton Camp. It was not used to transport soldiers; they always had to march to the Camp. It ran from Milford Station, to the Lichfield Road where there was a crossing. The trains only ran in daylight hours, because of the hazard, but during those hours a soldier with a red flag was always on duty to warn road users, or halt the train if necessary. The railway ran across the common, through the grounds of Sister Dora Convalescent Home, up a cutting by the Golf Club House and onward to the top of the Chase.

Not long after all these changes, mother and I were invited to tea with Elizabeth Mort who lived in one of the railway cottages at Milford. Her husband William worked on the railway and he had warned his wife that a troop train would be coming within a few moments of our arrival. It was carrying wounded soldiers, mainly stretcher cases to the Camp Hospital.

"We have not been allowed to talk about it" Elizabeth told us, "They do not want a crowd". Several Army and Red Cross Ambulances had arrived and as soon as the train drew slowly into the station the medical staff began their work.

Railway Cottages, Milford

About a dozen people had also gathered to see what was happening. I was so upset to see the state of some of the men, they had been transported to Milford straight from the trenches, and they were in a pitiful condition. One lady suggested I should not get upset, "There is a war on" but I knew that they were someone's father or son and they all looked so sad.

Poor Elizabeth Mort. She did not know what was to come. Her eldest son Paul was lost at sea on 8th February, 1917. He was serving on HMS Ghurka, a destroyer, built in 1907 for the Royal Navy when she was sunk after hitting a German mine. Only five of the crew survived.[16]. They were pulled from the sea covered in oil by the armed trawler Highlander. Seventy-five men were lost.

---

[16] *The wreck is located at a depth of 30 metres off Dungeness It is designated as a "protected place" under the Protection of Military Remains act 1986*

HMS Ghurka

We did our bit to help the soldiers. Often on a twelve-mile route march, the officers would choose to take a break of about thirty minutes, outside our house. We kept a new tin bath to take out, filled it with six gallons of water and provided a few cups. A drink was certainly needed, as there would be another four miles march back to camp. When the soldiers came marching by there was always a group of small boys bringing up the rear and trying very hard to keep up and keep in step!

We were also asked if we could entertain some of our own troops who were stationed on the Chase. We had regular visits from a Corporal and a Sergeant. In civilian life the Corporal was a coachman to a family living in West Ealing. The Sergeant told us he worked in Hartley's Jam Factory and that he made the wooden pips they put in raspberry jam! Of course we didn't believe him but he did not deviate from his story and we were unable to get any further information from him. After the war the Corporal wrote to say they had both survived and were back home working at their old jobs.

Mrs Trundley was living alone in her home and so she was asked to let her sitting room and two bedrooms to a Camp Officer named Sandys who had three children. When the eldest children started school I walked them down the lane with me. They were with Mrs Trundley for over a year.

Workmen on the Camp

Sometimes it was difficult to sleep. In the winter mock fighting took place from about nine o'clock until three in the morning. It was a terrible noise; the whole area would be alight, with guns going off and bangs of one sort or another. It must have been unbearable in Brocton.

There was often noise and fighting from drunks while the camp was being built, to such an extent that in February 1915 all the public houses surrounding Cannock Chase, including the Golf Club, had to close at 9 p.m. Unfortunately, this did not solve the problem, and in August the Landlords of the Barley Mow at Milford and the Chetwynd Arms at Brocton gave an undertaking that they would not sell beer in bottles to be taken off the premises. Mr Whitehouse, the landlord of the Seven Stars, was also asked to give a similar undertaking. Although he was aware that there was a terrible problem with construction workers getting so drunk that they were unable to work the next morning, he was not happy. Eventually it was agreed that he would not serve anyone from the Camp but he could continue to serve locals if he recognised them!

Things got much better when the Navvies eventually moved on and the Military were left to control the soldiers. At last the ladies of the Parish felt able to go out of an evening once again.

There were many sad days during the war but I clearly remember a happy occasion at the very start of hostilities. The Vicar, the Rev. Thomas Busher, announced in September 1914 that he would be leaving the parish and moving to Carisbrooke on the Isle of Wight. However, he would never forget Berkswich, as he was taking something very special with him to his new parish. He then announced his engagement to Alice May Twigg, always known as May, of Weeping Cross House.

They were married on Wednesday, 14th October, 1914 at 11 o'clock in Baswich Church. The wedding was supposed to be a quiet affair as the Bride's father, Henry, had died earlier in the year. Only relatives and very close friends had been invited to the service but the Church was full. Parishioners had turned out in force and the whole school was allowed to wait outside to see the happy couple. May was wearing a grey and mauve costume and carried a bouquet of white lilies. It would be the last time we would see the couple, as they would be leaving for their honeymoon in Worthing, and then go straight on to Carisbrooke.[17] The teachers and pupils had given them a silver cake-basket as a wedding present and they had lots of other gifts from grateful parishioners. Would the new vicar be held in such esteem we all wondered?

Although this was a happy day, the couple would face sadness before the end of the war. On 24th September 1918 Frank Twigg, May's brother was killed. In January 1920, after the intervention of Sir John Twigg, a distant relative, Frank's body was exhumed from its isolated grave and brought to the

---

[17] *From 1914 Princess Beatrice the youngest daughter of Queen Victoria was living in Carisbrooke Castle. Beatrice became a great friend of the Busher's and was God-mother to their daughter Rosemary.*

Frank Twigg

British Cemetery at Bellicourt.[18] The letter, from the Imperial War Graves Commission, informing the family of Franks new burial place states that "The re-burial has been carefully and reverently carried out." Frank had been an excellent sportsman, playing Hockey and Cricket for Staffordshire.

By 1919 the family home, Weeping Cross House, and all its contents were for sale. The Twigg family were finally to leave the Parish of Berkswich after living in the area for centuries.

---

[18] *Bellicourt British Cemetery now contains 1,204 burials and commemorations of the First World War. 313 of the burials are unidentified but there are special memorials to 21 casualties known or believed to be buried among them.*

Chapter 5
Mrs Annie Longson, School Teacher.

The children had walked from school in a long crocodile this Monday afternoon to stand with respect around the Memorial. My husband, William, led the way whilst I brought up the rear. I can remember many of the young men whose names are inscribed on the memorial. They were my pupils at school not so many years ago. How could I forget young Robert Coates, such a smart lad who joined the Coldstream Guards? He was killed in action in September 1916, just nineteen year old.[19] His mother has been the school cleaner since 1913 and she is an absolute gem, always on time despite the walk from her home on Stockton Common, and making an excellent job of keeping the school spick and span. Since the death of her husband in 1917, she desperately needs the meagre £1.11s.3d a week we pay her.

Mr & Mrs Longson

---

[19] *Robert Coates is buried in Grove Town Cemetery, Meaulte, where 1,395 soldiers who lost their lives on the Somme are buried.*

Young Fred Hawkins had also been a pupil at our school and made us very proud when in 1918 he was awarded the Military Medal for Gallant Conduct in the firing line. He had brought several men to safety during a period of heavy shelling. Wounded himself on three occasions, but, he was keen to return to the Front after a spell back home with his father at Hazelstrine.

William and I came to Walton in January 1892 from Urmston, Lancashire. We had been married just a month earlier when William heard of his appointment at Walton and learnt that the position came with a cottage situated just next door to the school. William had undertaken two years training at St Paul's College Cheltenham and had been teaching for just four years. St Paul's College had been founded as "an Institution for the training of masters and mistresses upon scriptural and evangelical principles in connection with the Church of England" so it was natural that he should be successful in obtaining a post in a Church School. The fact that he could play the piano and harmonium was also in his favour.

I had been a trainee teacher in Urmston, Manchester but it was not until May 1895 that I was officially appointed to the staff of the school, although I had helped out from time to time when necessary.[20] It is with great regret that we have no children of our own so the school has become our life and, apart from William taking long walks over the Chase or along the canal with our two black Labrador dogs - his gun tucked under his arm, our days revolve around our pupils.

Now, in 1920, things are at last getting better but the war years have been very difficult. We were constantly trying to raise money, first for iron fencing to go around the school and then for a piano. Fund raising events were always a great success but there was just one drawback - the school was the only building in the village big enough for dancing or for a whist

---

[20] *Staffordshire Record Office D 3361/14/12*

drive. Each time a social was arranged, all the desks and chairs had to be moved into the playground!

This created a great deal of work and delayed the start of lessons on the following day. A request for a tarpaulin sheet to go over the equipment while it was standing in the playground was turned down due to expense. We just had to hope it didn't rain! By November 1915 these social events had become a regular occurrence at the school. Normally we would start at around 8 p.m. with a Whist Drive, often with as many as 31 tables. At 10 p.m. the tables would be cleared away for dancing to the music of the piano occasionally accompanied by a violin. The evenings closed at midnight with the singing of the National Anthem. It was good to see so many soldiers from the camps joining us at these social gatherings.

There was also no money available to provide Zeppelin Air Raid insurance. Just what would have happened if we had been hit I don't know. The Parish Council did, however, have a plan to protect us if such a raid should happen. A bell on each of the following buildings, Baswich Church, Walton Church, Milford Hall and Brocton Lodge, would be tolled three times, then a pause, and then three more rings. This was to be repeated for five minutes. At this warning parishioners were to extinguish all lights in their homes[21].

We were not hit by Zeppelins, but we were hit, in the early hours of Sunday 7th May 1916, by a motor car that failed to negotiate the curve in the road as it travelled towards Stafford. By this time we had smart iron railings around the playground but there were large brick pillars either side of the gate by the big oak tree. The car had completely demolished them and, on Monday, William's first job was to remove the debris so that the pupils could get into school. Just what happened I don't know but William damaged his right hand and for several weeks he was unable to write. I had to make entries in the School Log

---

[21] *Parish Council minutes, 23rd March 1916*

Book for him. He was also unable to write on the blackboard or to play the organ at Baswich Church for morning service - something he always enjoyed doing.

Mr Longson with some of his pupils in front of Walton School

As the war progressed, the Vicar and Captain Levett wished to instil into the pupils a sense of pride in our country. The Vicar presented us with a Union Jack, and Captain Levett provided a flagpole. After school one November afternoon in 1916, the flag was unfurled as the children gathered round in the playground. After prayers led by the Vicar, remembering former pupils of the school who were now in France, and praying for their safety, the flag was saluted and the National Anthem sung.

1916 also saw the official instigation of Empire Day on 24th May, which had been Queen Victoria's birthday. It was set up by Irish Peer, the Earl of Meath, to remind children that they formed part of the British Empire, and that they might think, with others in lands across the sea, what it meant to be sons and daughters of such a glorious Empire. The strength of the Empire depended upon them, and they must never forget it. In 1917 the children held a collection for Lord Meath's fund to send cigarettes to our troops in France.

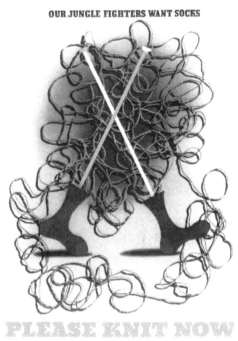

OUR JUNGLE FIGHTERS WANT SOCKS

PLEASE KNIT NOW

FOR INFORMATION PATTERNS AND WOOL APPLY TO

As time went by, food became scarce. At the start of the war, people who could afford it went around panic buying food and hoarding it at home. By the end of August 1914 some shops had completely sold out of food! Eventually people realised that they could only eat so much, and things returned almost to normal until 1917 when the Germans started submarine warfare. Ships bringing grain from Canada and the USA were sunk with great regularity, and this had an immediate impact on our food supplies.

We had run a gardening club at the school for some years, and the boys grew vegetables under the watchful eyes of Mr Dix, from Weeping Cross House. The boys had their plots on the land in front of the Parish Rooms at the top of School Lane. In 1916 Mr Dix left the area and Mr Enoch Pierce,

gardener at Milford Hall, became our official gardening instructor. He came regularly to advise the children and help them keep a written record of their crops. Their efforts at growing vegetables helped feed their families, and was much appreciated by their mothers. A school inspector would come regularly from Stafford to see how things were growing and check that the boys were learning, rather than just escaping lessons.

As a Church school, we were regularly scrutinized by the Diocesan Inspector who came and sat in on our scripture lessons. Fortunately we always seemed to get a glowing report. The Vicar also visited most weeks, one of his duties being to check that the registers had been completed correctly! In March 1915, as it became clear that the war would go on for some time and it was important to preserve our food supplies, I spent two days in the Education Department in Stafford with other teachers, learning how to instruct the girls in cookery. In April, it was decided that cookery should be placed on the curriculum, and the classes began at the beginning of June. Ten older girls and I occupied the Parish Room and I passed my cookery know how on to them. They made wholemeal bread, cakes and scones. Dinners were provided on three days a week. If the Parish Room was being used for other activities, the older girls used the kitchen in our home next door to the school, to prepare the meals. By 1917 there was a desperate shortage of bread, which was part of the staple diet of poorer families. I noticed that children who brought their dinners to school invariably brought bread, and I estimated that over 120 lbs of bread were used for dinners each week. I decided that we must provide a cooked meal for our students every day. For 10d per week and 8d for the younger children, we were able to provide soup or stew and dumplings followed by a milk pudding. A letter was sent by the County Secretary to the National War Savings Committee, telling them about our scheme. I was delighted when I was informed of their reply which stated "This case is one of the most notable achievements we have had the pleasure of recording".[22] Once again I was called to Stafford to be informed that we must encourage our pupils to make their own bread and to be sure that not a scrap was wasted. Bakers were forbidden to bake any but Government regulation bread. This was made from various ingredients, including barley, rice, maize, oatmeal and in October 1917 they were permitted to add potatoes in the proportion of 1lb to 7 lbs of flour. It also became an offence to throw rice at a wedding! In July, when it looked like we would have a glut of fruit, the school was closed for the day and the grown-ups were invited to attend a demonstration of fruit bottling by Mrs Ward, a farmers wife from Lichfield.

It was also my place to see that all the girls could knit and sew. One of our favourite sewing tasks was to make a pair of mittens from a rabbit pelt. By December 1914 the pupils, with the help of the teachers, had made 4 nightshirts, 15 pairs of socks (with another 12 pairs nearly finished), 18 body belts, 20 scarves, 5 helmets, 6 pairs of gloves and 15 pairs of mittens. Several of these items were sent directly to old pupils who were at the Front or in training. The rest were sent to the Honourable Mrs Allsopp at Walton Bury or Mrs Levett at Milford Hall to be forwarded to the Red Cross. The boys and younger girls helped the war effort by unravelling old knitted items, rewinding the wool, and then knitting simple mittens for the soldiers to wear in the trenches.

---

[22] *Stafford Newsletter 19th May 1917*

The children were doing all they could to help, but the demand for warm clothes and equipment continued to rise. We held a meeting in School in June 1915 to which we invited parents to see what they could do to further help the men at the front. It was decided to hold a weekly working party in the Parish Rooms to make sandbags. These were urgently needed at the front and Casualty Stations. It was also agreed that a working party would be set up in Brocton, or bags could be made at home if mothers were unable to attend the working parties. Each sandbag cost 7d. Everyone was encouraged to come and help.

September 1915 saw the establishment of another school in the area. George and Elizabeth Osborn had bought Weeping Cross House and opened a small preparatory boarding school for boys. It was called "Baswich House School". Although we did not lose any pupils when this school opened, we did seem to lose - at least temporarily - some of our post. After several months of wrongly delivered post it was agreed to write to the Education Committee and ask them to address all correspondence to "The Headmaster, Berkswich C of E School, Walton", instead of just to "Baswich School", to obviate any confusion with Baswich House School, Weeping Cross.

Our pupils did not come from such affluent homes as the boys who attend Baswich House School. Many came from large families with seven or eight children, and walked to school from as far afield as Hazelstrine, Tixall, Brancote and Brocton. Perhaps it was one of the saddest days of my teaching life when five of our pupils, the Roper's, from Stockton Lane, were taken into the workhouse in 1914.

I had a store of shoes and clothes and often, on wet or snowy days, many of the children were dressed in an odd assortment of garments while I made sure their own clothes were dry and warm before they made the journey home. If the weather was really bad, particularly when there had been heavy snow, the attendance at school was poor. Sometimes there were so few pupils in school that we sent them all home until the weather improved. I remember on one occasion, I think it was in 1916, only eight pupils made it to school. All of them lived close by in Walton Village. When the weather is particularly cold and wet, I have a large jug of hot cocoa ready to help warm up those children who walk long distances to school.

No wonder parents were not keen to send their children to school in such circumstances as, during the early years of the war, the school heating system left a lot to be desired. In January 1917 the average temperature at 9 a.m. was just 39° Fahrenheit (3.5° Centigrade). On 6th February the temperature inside school was only just above freezing. There was nothing for it, but to close the school until a new part could be acquired for the boiler - not an easy task, as all production of castings was devoted to the war effort. It took three weeks before the part could be obtained and the repair completed. By then there had been a considerable improvement in the weather[23]!

It was a wonder that the children ever learnt anything. Holidays were given on several Holy Days, including, Ash Wednesday, St Thomas' Day and

Wilmot Martin

[23] *Berkswich School Log Book*

Ascension Day so that they could attend church at Baswich. When the Director of Education, Graham Balfour, received a knighthood in the King's Birthday Honours in 1917 there was a day off for the children, and the induction of a new vicar was another reason for a holiday!

The school was often used for social events such as the annual rummage sale, County Council elections, or a concert. All such events meant an extra day's holiday. Villagers always enjoyed the concerts put on in the school two or three times a year, by Wilmot Martin, a farmer from Hixon, who became known as the "Staffordshire Harry Lauder". He started touring the area with his small concert party during the war to raise funds for Belgian refugees and the Red Cross, and over the years raised thousands for charity.

The Davis Girls dressed ready to perform in "Enchanted Glen"

Our Annual Social Gathering for school funds on New Year's Eve, 1918, was something special as it was the first time since the end of the war that we had reason to celebrate. Tea was served at 5.30 p.m. and the building was bursting at the seams as everyone wanted to join in the fun. After tea there was the usual whist drive, followed by dancing until the clock struck twelve. The music was provided by Mrs Clara and Miss Martha Stichling. Mrs Stichling was German and had

(c) Berkswich History Society

come to Britain with her German husband in about 1882. Their daughter, Martha, had started a dancing school for girls in 1907, and in 1917 her pupils performed in a show entitled "Enchanted Glen" at the prisoner of war camp on Cannock Chase. Martha was well known for providing entertainment at garden parties, fetes, and charity events and of course her pupils, many of them from Brocton, enjoyed showing off the dances they had learnt.

The Prisoner of War Camp had opened in April 1917 under the command of Lt. Colonel Sir Alfred Grant, Bart. of Moneymusk in Aberdeenshire. Sir Arthur had been in the Gordon Highlanders until he was wounded in the arm in June 1915. He returned to the UK to convalesce before taking up his post at Brocton. On his appointment he made a point of calling on his neighbours in an attempt to get to know them all. It was quite a shock for some locals when they opened the door to a fellow kitted out in full Highland dress. Arthur Grant was to become a very close friend of Captain and Mrs Levett and for the duration of his stay in Staffordshire he rented "The Leys" in Brocton Village for his wife and large family.

A "Victory Treat" was held for the school children in February 1919. The celebrations started with a service in church at 2.30 p.m. and then they were

Sir Arthur Grant and his wife Evelyn

entertained in school by a gramophone! Tea was followed by a Punch & Judy show provided by Professor Steel.

At 7 p.m. the children departed clutching a bun, an orange and a bag of sweets!

Many a time the school had to be closed for weeks at a time when there were epidemics of childhood diseases. Outbreaks of measles and scarlet fever occurred regularly. Poor William Northwood was knocked down by a car a couple of years ago, and taken to the hospital to recover from his injuries. However, he contracted scarlet fever in the hospital! Scarlet fever could mean a stay in hospital of six or seven weeks without any visitors at all. There were also regular cases of diphtheria amongst the pupils. Nurse Lyons visited the school every three months to check on the health of the children. She was often the one to notice the first signs of infection in a child, as parents were very reluctant to call out the doctor. Such a visit could cost half a week's wages for some poor families.

The Autumn Term of 1918 was quite extraordinary. School opened on 2nd September after the Hay and Corn Harvest holiday. Food was still desperately short so, on 9th September, children from Standards III – VII went out for the whole day, gathering blackberries with their teachers. The same thing happened three days the following week. Five more days in September were spent the same way. On the 1st & 4th October pupils were again out looking for blackberries. The following week, school was closed for potato picking and on 15th it was blackberries again!

In the autumn of 1918, children and wounded soldiers throughout the country were picking blackberries for jam making at the request of the Food Production Department. A target of 6 tons was required from the area around Colwich, which included Berkswich!

Injured soldiers picking blackberries

By 23rd October there were sixty-three pupils absent with influenza. On the orders of the Medical Officer, concerned by the increasing number of deaths from the disease, the school was closed until 6th November. On 11th November the Armistice was signed and an afternoon holiday was granted. Two further days holiday were given the following week, described as "War Holiday"! The 'flu epidemic showed no sign of abating and so, on 10th December the school was closed once again on medical advice until 6th January[24].

Despite all these closures the children did learn, and the school received glowing reports at each Inspection. I am sure that all the young men educated in Berkswich School were a credit to our community while they were fighting for their country. It is so sad that they did not all return.

---

[24] *The children attended school for 31 days out of a possible 77 during the term.*

Chapter 6
Harry Malpass, Farmer

It has been a rush to get the milking done this afternoon so that I can attend the dedication of the War Memorial, but I've made it just in time.

Mr & Mrs Malpass

We have lived at Walton Farm, owned by Captain Levett, since 1915 when we took over the tenancy. The farmhouse faces the high brick wall surrounding Walton Bury and so has no view whatsoever. However, we have an enormous barn that can be seen for miles around. From the rickyard we can look towards the Chase - a wonderful view, especially now that the rows of Army huts have disappeared from the skyline. They are now reappearing in the nearby villages, painted and spruced up to become homes for families or village halls for local communities.

Originally the farm had been mostly arable but we have, since the outbreak of war, gone over to dairy, sheep and pigs. By 1916 the Army had requisitioned over half a million privately owned horses for military service in France. Without a heavy horse it was impossible to plough the stony ground of Walton Farm so the move to dairy was the best solution. A tractor was beyond my means in 1916. I love horses, and as soon as the war was over, I returned to my hobby of breeding Shires. We have also acquired a Cavalry horse named Robert. He is rather nervous, especially on the roads, but is happy to be ridden or do any sort of farm work. The Army, realising that it was expensive to feed the horses that they no longer needed soon put them up for sale. I went to a big sale in Shrewsbury just before Christmas 1918 to see if they had any animals I would be interested in. That's when I bought Robert.

Farming in Berkswich

My wife, Elizabeth, whom I married in 1913, takes care of the poultry. She is a farmer's daughter; her parents William and Florence Edwards have the tenancy of nearby Stockton Farm, another of Captain Levett's properties. The Captain also owns Weeping Cross Farm at the top of Baswich Lane and Home Farm, directly opposite Milford Hall. Home Farm is also a dairy farm, run by foreman John Humphreys, a Welshman who married local girl Alice Simpson. Alice takes care of the Dairy which is opposite their home, Dairy Cottage, and she makes cheese and butter with milk from the cows.

Walton Farm Barn

My day usually starts about 5.30 a.m. The cows are milked by hand, the milk strained and then left to cool in the Dairy before being put into 17-gallon milk churns. During the war, and right up until last year when all the soldiers finally left, I would load the milk onto the float and we would journey down Brocton Lane and then up Chase Road to deliver the milk to the Army Camp. It was a struggle for the pony to pull the loaded float up Chase Road but the return to Walton carrying only yesterday's empty churns was no problem at all. During the summer this was always a pleasant trip but winter was quite different. Often it was so cold, especially on the top of the Chase that I had to wear two overcoats over my thick winter sweaters. With so many soldiers on the Chase, there was always a ready market for our milk but, as winter approaches, I am glad I no longer have to make that journey every morning.

Now I go to Milford Station where the churns are loaded on to the 8.30 a.m. train and taken to the Midland Counties Dairy in Birmingham - a much easier journey for the pony! We also sell milk locally. Most villagers will walk up to the farm with a large jug when they require milk, and sometimes enterprising young boys will earn a few coppers by delivering it directly to regular local customers. Milk is 2d a quart and Elizabeth sells her eggs 10 for a 1/-.

We had to work hard during the war as all the fit men had been called up. If I needed help I had to make do with the Women's Land Army![25] Although the girls were doing a very valuable job, the government found it necessary to issue the following warning to them – "You are doing a man's work and so you are dressed rather like a man; but remember that because you wear a smock and trousers you should take care to behave like an English girl who expects chivalry and respect from everyone she meets." What would we have done without the girls? I remember reading in one of my farming magazines that in a survey completed in 1918 there were nearly four thousand girls working in the fields, over five and a half

---

[25] *The Women's Land Army was formed in 1917. Britain had only 3 weeks of food supply in the UK left when the Women's Land Army was formed, with a helping hand from a Lady Trudie Denman, who had her part to play in WW1 but is more well known for her efforts in WW2.*

thousand milking our cows, as well as those employed as carters, thatchers, ploughmen, tractor drivers and shepherds.

Land Girls

Before the Government set up the Land Army we had done our bit as a community. Women who were prepared to help on the land had to leave their details with Mrs Bates at "Roycroft", on the Main Road at Walton. Any farmers wanting help just had to contact Mrs Bates and she would, if at all possible, put you in touch with a willing volunteer.

"Roycroft" had been from 1911 until the outbreak of war, the home of Edward Harvie and his wife. Edward had come to Stafford from London to work as an Electrical Engineer and at first he lodged at Rose Cottage, close to Roycroft. When he married he moved next door with his lovely new wife Mabel. Before long they had a baby boy, Geoffrey I think he was called and then in November 1914 Edward enlisted in the Army. He was killed in November 1916[26]. His wife had by this time gone home to her parents in Surrey and the Bates family moved into "Roycroft"

Throughout the war we still had the regular journey to fetch coal. Two of us would go with horse and cart to Littleton Colliery to fetch the coal directly from the pithead, a slow journey of around nine miles. When we had a new delivery I let old Mrs Jemima Trundley have a few hundred-weight. She pays me when she can. I feel I must do a little to help her as she is all alone in the world.

The war really hit home when news came that Leonard Tilstone, son of Harry Tilstone, Captain Levett's gamekeeper, had been killed in July 1916. Harry is treated as one of the family up at the Hall and over the years I have often see him going over the fields with young master Dick during the school holidays.

The Tilstone's live in Cressell Cottage[27], a six-roomed cottage on the Milford Estate, right in the centre of the land we overlook from the top of Walton Hill. Harry and Harriet Tilstone did have two daughters and six sons. Five of the boys went off to war and four of them have returned. Only Colin, who was just eight when war broke out, was left at home along with his two sisters. Colin, with his "Gang", Bill Dawson, Tom Alcorn, Sidney Clay & Co. could often be seen roaming round the fields amusing themselves by knocking old tins off tree stumps and fence posts with either their slings or catapults. They were very proficient with their homemade weapons.

---

[26] *The Thiepval Memorial, the Memorial to the Missing of the Somme, bears the names of more than 72,000 officers and men of the United Kingdom and South African forces who died in the Somme sector before 20 March 1918 and have no known grave. Over 90% of those commemorated died between July and November 1916. The memorial also serves as an Anglo-French Battle Memorial in recognition of the joint nature of the 1916 offensive and a small cemetery containing equal numbers of Commonwealth and French graves lies at the foot of the memorial.*
[27] *Now known as Chapel Leasowes*

1916 proved to be a terrible year for the Tilstone family. Violet, their youngest daughter, was thirteen when she contracted scarlet fever; she was admitted to hospital and, by some strange turn of events, developed appendicitis while there. She died in April following an operation to remove her appendix. They had barely recovered from the shock of Violet's death when, in July, there was news that Leonard had been killed. Leonard[28] lost his life in India so there is no prospect of his parents every being able to visit his grave. I am sure the

family will have received every support from the Levetts as Harry had been in their service, first as a carpenter and then as gamekeeper, for well over twenty years.

There was further sadness to come as Gwendoline, their eldest daughter, was also to leave. In 1918 she married Frank Noyer, a New Zealander who had been stationed on the Chase. On Christmas Day 1918 she set sail for Wellington without her husband, on the Union-Castle Mail Steamship "Briton", with over fifty other new wives of New Zealand soldiers. Their husbands would follow when the Army decided they should!

Harry Tilstone with a troublesome swan.

[28] *The Kirkee Memorial commemorates more than 1,800 servicemen who died in India during the First World War, who are buried in civil and cantonment cemeteries in India and Pakistan where their graves can no longer be properly maintained.*

By the beginning of 1918, food supplies were very low and Stafford Food Control Committee introduced strict rules regarding the purchase of some commodities. From Monday, 25th February, tea was rationed at one and a quarter ounces per person per week. Butter or margarine was limited to 4 ounces per person per week. Meat was also rationed. It was necessary to register with just one butcher, and you were allowed to purchase meat to the value of 1/3d per head. Failure to utilise your ration during the appointed week meant that it was lost. It could not be carried over to the following week! Each purchase had to be marked off on the appropriate portion of the food card. Should you have the misfortune to die, your ration book was to be returned to the Authorities within three days!

During the previous year the Game Laws were relaxed. It became illegal to feed game birds on corn or maize and game was no longer protected. Anyone could shoot the pheasants or any other game on the land of which they are the tenant. This was to provide food for humans and also to prevent the birds from eating precious crops in the fields. In an attempt to save even more food all the hunting packs had been shot and we were encouraged to shoot the foxes to prevent them taking poultry. It also became an offence to adopt and feed stray dogs, these creatures had to be handed over to the police, and no doubt they were then disposed of.

The maximum price we farmers could charge for milk was restricted in April 1918 to 2/- per gallon. Then from May to September, when the grass was growing and the cows producing more, the price fell to 1/6 per gallon.

It was different for our soldiers, one young man, Billy Walker, wrote home in April 1918 saying "*I expect you envy us our rations. We get two good meat meals a day (exclusive of bacon for breakfast) and our daily meat ration almost equates to the civilian weekly one.*"

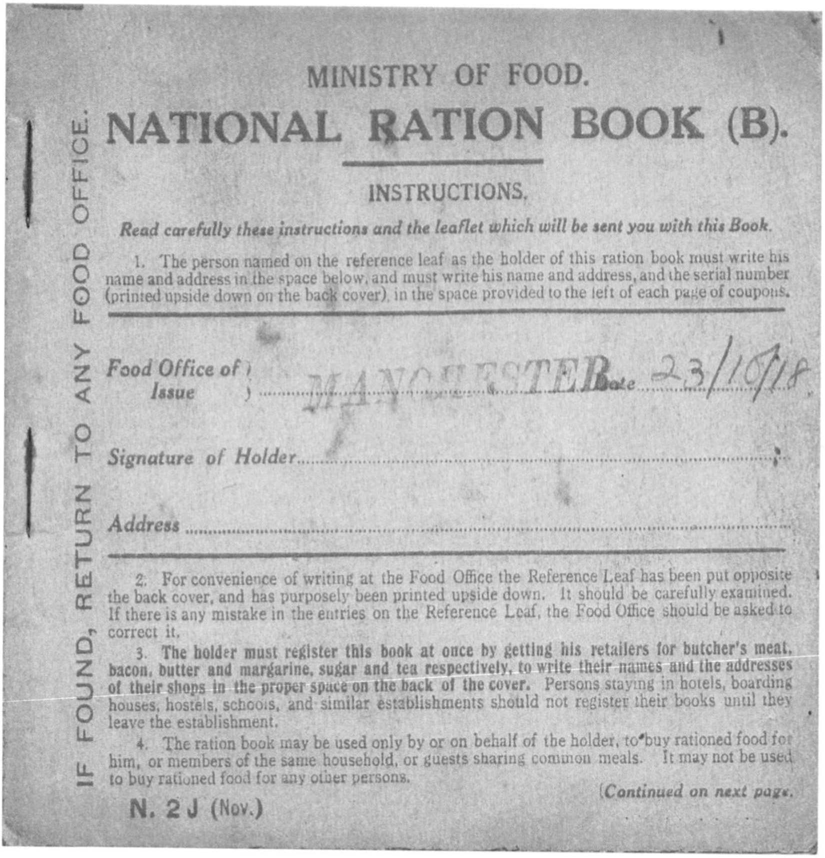
IF FOUND, RETURN TO ANY FOOD OFFICE.

MINISTRY OF FOOD.

NATIONAL RATION BOOK (B).

INSTRUCTIONS.

Read carefully these instructions and the leaflet which will be sent you with this Book.

1. The person named on the reference leaf as the holder of this ration book must write his name and address in the space below, and must write his name and address, and the serial number (printed upside down on the back cover), in the space provided to the left of each page of coupons.

Food Office of Issue MANCHESTER Date 23/10/18

Signature of Holder..................

Address..................

2. For convenience of writing at the Food Office the Reference Leaf has been put opposite the back cover, and has purposely been printed upside down. It should be carefully examined. If there is any mistake in the entries on the Reference Leaf, the Food Office should be asked to correct it.

3. **The holder must register this book at once by getting his retailers for butcher's meat, bacon, butter and margarine, sugar and tea respectively, to write their names and the addresses of their shops in the proper space on the back of the cover.** Persons staying in hotels, boarding houses, hostels, schools, and similar establishments should not register their books until they leave the establishment.

4. The ration book may be used only by or on behalf of the holder, to buy rationed food for him, or members of the same household, or guests sharing common meals. It may not be used to buy rationed food for any other persons.

[Continued on next page.

N. 2 J (Nov.)

1918 Ration Book

By April 1919 things were slightly better and, if you required extra sugar for preserving fruit or jam making you could make an application to your regular supplier, stating how much extra you required and pledging to use it only for preserving! Unfortunately, there was nowhere near enough to meet demand as Staffordshire was allocated just 30 tons for the whole of the county. No-one, no matter who they were, would get more than 28lbs of extra sugar!

DEFENCE OF THE REALM. E.P. 6.

MINISTRY OF FOOD.

BREACHES OF THE RATIONING ORDER

The undermentioned convictions have been recently obtained:–

Court	Date	Nature of Offence	Result
HENDON - -	29th Aug., 1918	Unlawfully obtaining and using ration books -	3 Months' Imprisonment
WEST HAM -	29th Aug., 1918	Being a retailer & failing to detach proper number of coupons	Fined £20
SMETHWICK -	22nd July, 1918	Obtaining meat in excess quantities - - -	Fined £50 & £5 5s. costs
OLD STREET -	4th Sept., 1918	Being a retailer selling to unregistered customer	Fined £72 & £5 5s. costs
OLD STREET -	4th Sept., 1918	Not detaching sufficient coupons for meat sold -	Fined £25 & £2 2s. costs
CHESTER-LE-STREET	4th Sept., 1918	Being a retailer returning number of registered customers in excess of counterfoils deposited - - - -	Fined £50 & £3 3s. costs
HIGH WYCOMBE	7th Sept., 1918	Making false statement on application for and using Ration Books unlawfully - · · - · · ·	Fined £40 & £6 4s. costs

Enforcement Branch, Local Authorities Division,
MINISTRY OF FOOD. September, 1918.

Food supplies are slowly getting back to normal now, thanks to us farmers, although butter and sugar are to remain rationed a little longer. So many people round here grow their own vegetables and keep chickens that I suppose we haven't really felt the hardship like folks in the cities have. I am sure no-one locally has been driven to cheat the system like some!

Chapter 7
Margaret Smallwood of Brocton.

I was ten when war broke out and all of a sudden life in Brocton changed. It had always been a peaceful place.

The Smallwood family.
Margaret is standing behind her father

The war had hardly started before news came that Lionel Hughes[29] had been killed, the first boy from the Parish to lose his life. I only knew him by sight as he lived in one of the "big posh" houses in the village called "The Warren" and he had been away at school, Lancing College. His father owned a

---

[29] *Lionel is buried in Ration Farm Military Cemetery about 2.5 kms south of the village of La Chapelle-d'Armentieres*

factory in the Potteries and he was an only child. Everyone said what a nice boy he was, so athletic, playing football, cricket and running for the College as well as shooting at Bisley.

He went out to France in September 1914, and was killed by a stray shell on 29th October whilst the Battalion were attempting to remove the large number of German bodies that had built up in front of the trench. His parents were heart broken and he was just nineteen.

As a family we are almost self-sufficient, growing all our own vegetables and having our own sheep, pigs, hens and cows. Every Friday mother makes butter to last us the week as well as baking bread.

The sheep and cows are turned out on to Cannock Chase, where they roam freely until about four in the afternoon. When I was still at school, it was my job, on arriving home, to round up the cows and bring them back for milking. Usually they had munched their way towards Milford. Before the outbreak of war, my father, Alfred, had been summoned to appear in Court[30] for allowing his sheep to stray onto the Stafford to Lichfield road at Milford. Father claimed that the road passed over Common Land, and therefore it was not an offence. The case had to be adjourned so that the Police could check the legal position, and it all caused quite a stir in the Village. Counsel's opinion was sought by the Chief Constable and, eventually, the case was withdrawn. Although there had been many complaints from cyclists and motor car drivers about the animals, and some people suggested that the Golf Club had also complained, it was found that, as the land was not fenced on both sides, it was not an offence[31] to allow stock to pass over it. Once the war started, and the railway was built from Milford Station across the Common, we then had to make sure the cattle were kept well out of the way

---

[30] *Lichfield Mercury 16th September 1910*
[31] *Section 25 of Highways Act 1864*

Club House and Green on Cannock Chase

The Golf Club strongly denied complaining about our sheep and cattle, as they did no more harm that the deer that roamed freely on the Chase. Mr Hutchings, the Golf Professional, had a lot more to complain about when the War Office decided to build a railway across his Golf Course.

The track cut right through the fifth hole as well as causing general wear and tear all across the course. It is surprising that the club has managed to survive. The railway was dismantled in 1918, but the Camps remained a little longer. The officers of the 3rd Highland Brigade were allowed to use the course and, when they left the area in 1919, they presented the Club with a wonderful trophy - the "Highland Brigade Bowl"

Once the work started on the Camps, our quiet little village became a hive of activity. Every day we would hear the bugler play Reveille at 6 a.m. and lights out at 11 p.m. each night. Mother decided to make the most of things and opened a little shop in one room of our house to cater for the needs of the many workmen and soldiers who regularly passed our house.

We sold cigarettes, cakes, sweets, pork pies, minerals, fruit in season, and, when we could get them - bananas.

Each morning a German Officer, accompanied by a British guard, would come to collect milk for the Senior German Officer at the Prisoner of War Camp. If it wasn't ready, the two of them would stand and wait by the cowshed door chatting, while my father milked the cow. The German Prisoners did some useful work in the area; I remember them constructing the concrete lining to Oldacre Brook, near Bank Farm, and also labouring on local farms. With so many of our own men away fighting, their efforts were appreciated.

But not everyone felt the same way about the Germans. In 1918 the following letter, to the Commanding Officer of the Prisoner of War Camp at Brocton, was published in the Stafford Newsletter.

Dear Sir,

Today our shop was polluted by the presence of German Prisoners.

The writer of this letter was on active service during the first months of the war and saw much of the bestial methods of the Germans that he vowed under no circumstances would he knowingly have dealings with or show courtesy to a German again.

To save further annoyance to ourselves and also to the Englishmen who are compelled to escort them, we shall be obliged it you will place our shop out of bounds to all German prisoners, otherwise the next entrant will likely meet with something more than forcible words.

Yours faithfully,

H. Pyrah,
Managing Director."

Thank goodness not everyone thought like that! However, in July 1919 there was a commotion in the area when two German PoW's, Gustav Hohendoff and Johann Reuter, dressed in their prisoner working clothes[32], escaped from Brocton Camp The war had been over for eight months, so why they should decide to abscond now was a mystery. Perhaps they did not want to be repatriated, or perhaps they wanted to enjoy the National Peace Celebrations which were planned for 19th July!

Brocton Mission Room

---

[32] *Lichfield Mercury 18th July 1919*

To help with the war effort, villagers would meet regularly at the Mission Room and knit scarves, balaclavas, gloves and socks for the soldiers. We also had piles of papers which we cut into strips. These were then twisted round a stick to make coiled paper which was stuffed into pillow cases provided by Miss Chetwynd of Brocton Hall. These pillows were used at the hospital on the Chase - not quite the same as a feather pillow but at least the "stuffing" could be thrown out after each use.

When I was fourteen I left Walton school to help my mother with all the farm work. I was responsible for delivering milk round Brocton. Twice a day I would travel round the village in the trap with a big milk can and a pint measure. This was a job I had to do, even on Christmas day!

The Smallwood Home in Brocton

After they were married in 1873 my grandparents, Mary & Richard, rented Green Farm from the Chetwynd Estate. Poor Mary had thirteen children in fifteen years, so it is no surprise that she passed away, aged 42, just six months after the birth of her daughter Margaret Isabella. Grandfather died eight years later and my Uncle William took over the running of the farm with help from his younger brothers, including my father. Eventually, William married and my father moved to the house I live in now.

Uncle Frank came to live with us. By this time he was working as a Railway Porter but, when war broke out he enlisted in the Army. He joined the Veterinary Corps looking after the horses - his experience with animals on the farm had qualified him for this work. The horses had a terrible time, but it meant that Frank was not fighting on the Front Line and so returned home safely. To mark the dedication of the War Memorial, all soldiers from the Parish who made it back home have been presented with a beaker engraved with their name and the words, "Parish of Berkswich, For War Services".

Uncle George, the youngest brother in the family, was a gunner with the 182nd Brigade, Royal Field Artillery, and unfortunately he did not make it home. He was killed in May 1916[33].

Uncle Frank has also been presented with a silver salver engraved with the words "Presented to Corporal Smallwood by 13th Veterinary Officers Mess" in recognition of his work with the horses. Uncle Frank loved horses and he would have been

---

[33] *George in buried in Mazingarbe Communal Cemetery which contains 248 Commonwealth Graves and 2 Germans.*

so upset to see how some of them were treated here in Brocton. Every Friday and Saturday evening great numbers of soldiers wanted to travel into Stafford for an evening's drinking and entertainment. The buses just could not cope, so it was not unusual to see gangs of young men travelling on open carts being pulled by over worked animals. It became so bad that the Staffordshire Advertiser published a letter from Mrs Stuart who lived on Weeping Cross. She wrote

"Is there no-one in this district who is sufficiently a lover of horse, and at the same time with the necessary authority to take on efficient supervision of their welfare. If so let him stand on Radford Bank or any other point between Brocton and Stafford on a Friday evening or a Saturday afternoon and evening and see these poor over-worked, half-starved animals being ruthlessly flogged up and down that road until one dreads almost to see the bones come through the skin with each slash of the whip!

They are in many cases only fit for the slaughterer's and how fourteen or sixteen soldiers can have the face to get into a small float or waggonette and be dragged to and from Stafford by one of these obviously suffering animals is past my understanding.

But thank God it is seldom our men we see practising this heartless cruelty and indeed it was not noticeable until some months ago. We all know that horse feeding is a problem nowadays but there are many fine horses about showing what is possible but if a man cannot or will not be bothered to feed his horse properly then neither should he be allowed to work it especially in the unnecessary (though profitable) occupation of joy riding for our colonial troops.[34]

The black and white timbered building that used to be Brocton Post Office is next door to Green Farm and soldiers returning to camp in the dark, after a few drinks at the "Barley Mow" or the "Chetwynd Arms", had a favourite pastime. A water butt collected rain water from the roof of the adjoining barn, but the soldiers were not interested in the water. That was tipped unceremoniously onto the road. The butt was then carried up to the top of Chase Road, set on its side and given a push to send it rolling back to where it started from. A huge joke when one has had a pint or two! It was no wonder that the Military Police began to keep an eye on things at Brocton Green!

Brocton Old Post Office

---

[34] *Staffordshire Advertiser, 26th May 1918.*

Brocton Cross Roads always seems to cause trouble. Poor father was coming home along the Cannock Road one evening, driving a horse and cart with a load of coal he had collected from Littleton Colliery. A covered cart was approaching in the opposite direction. All of a sudden a motor car, travelling at between eight and ten miles an hour, passed father and tried to squeeze in before it hit the cart travelling from the direction of Stafford. The driver of the car, twenty year old Myrtle English, from Lichfield, did not quite make it. The rear of the car struck the horse's nose, not hurting but causing him to jump and land in a nearby ditch. The shaft of our cart was broken and of course there was coal all over the road!

Myrtle was charged with "Driving in a Manner Dangerous to the Public" and was found guilty, paying father 33/6d in costs.

Chetwynd Arms

On the same day, in the same Court, a New Zealand soldier was fined for riding his bike without lights at 11.30 p.m. on the Cannock Road, near the Chetwynd Arms[35].

---

[35] *Staffordshire Advertiser, 27th July 1918.*

Military Police at Brocton Green

Now in 1920 everything is quieter. The soldiers have gone, the furniture and huts from the camp are being sold, and the village is returning to normal. Perhaps there are a few more visitors to the area now as they come, often in their new motor cars, to enjoy the countryside.

Chapter 8
Dowager Lady Salt

Major John C.B. McFerran of Rickerscote Hall, Irish linen manufacturer, looked on as his wife Helen knelt and placed a wreath at the foot of the Memorial. The war had helped his business considerably. Once the aeroplanes of the Royal Flying Corps had proved their worth, the demand for linen increased. It was used as a covering for mainplanes, tailplanes, and fuselage surfaces. As more planes were built, more linen was required.

Rickerscote Hall

The Germans had invaded Belgium on 4th August 1914 and much of the flax used in Irish Linen came from the Low Countries. The invading forces had destroyed all the crops, and therefore the price of linen rocketed, helping to make John McFerran a wealthy man. He would, however, gladly have given up his business if it had meant saving the life of his eldest son Maurice. Maurice was just twenty when he was killed in the little village of Pozières, 6 kilometres north-east of the town of Albert on 21st March 1918[36].

The family had divided their time between their Irish home in Belfast and their home in Stafford so it was no surprise when Maurice joined No 7 Officer Cadet Battalion at French Furge Camp, Curragh, Ireland, on 29th May 1916. He was commissioned into the Royal Irish Rifles in September 1916. He had fought at the Battle of Messine, the 3rd Battle of Ypres and at Cambrai. His Colonel wrote to his parents "He has been working as my intelligence officer for some time and during the recent battle[37] he has done great work for me: this young lad was indefatigable in running about under all sort of fire and maintaining touch between me and the companies. I owe the success of the battalion in great measure to his energy and bravery."

At just twenty his Colonel was right in referring to Maurice as "this young lad". So many of the soldiers who died were just young lads.

Although they felt his death deeply his parents were very proud that their son had been awarded the Military Cross. The citation echoes the sentiments of his Colonel stating "For conspicuous gallantry and devotion to duty. During three days fighting he maintained touch between the leading companies and battalion HQ. He went four times to the front through a heavy barrage and brought back valuable information".

The wreath that was so tenderly placed on the memorial was also a token of love and respect from Helen's mother, the Dowager Lady Salt.

---

[36] *The Pozières Memorial relates to the period of crisis in March and April 1918 when the Allied Fifth Army was driven back by overwhelming numbers across the former Somme battlefields, and the months that followed before the Advance to Victory, which began on 8 August 1918. The Memorial commemorates over 14,000 casualties of the United Kingdom and 300 of the South African Forces who have no known grave and who died on the Somme from 21 March to 7 August 1918.*
[37] *Cambrai*

Lady Salt's house at Walton on the Hill

Now aged eighty, Lady Helen Salt had left her home in Walton on the Hill earlier in the year to live in London. She felt she could not face the journey back to Stafford when the weather was so cold and the days so short. She had come to the parish upon her marriage in 1861, and between 1863 and 1876 she had borne eleven children. Little Violet had died aged just seven months, Mary had died at thirty-seven after an operation, George had died of enteric fever while fighting in the Boer War, and now this last dreadful war had robbed her of her youngest son, Walter. Not content with taking her son, the war had also taken the lives of two of her grandsons, Charles Pollock and young Maurice McFerran within ten days of each other. For some reason Charles, who was training to be a lawyer like his father, does not appear on our memorial. Perhaps that is because he has a home in Berkshire and his father, Ernest Pollock, is rather important as the Member of Parliament for Warwick and Leamington, and also Solicitor General.

Job Farnsworth, also in his eighties, had been Lady Salt's gardener at Walton for many years. He too was to lose a grandson, Ernest, in 1916. Lady Salt knew Ernest well as he had lived with his grandfather in the tied cottage that she had built, so that he could travel to work each day as a Stock Clerk at Siemens works on the Lichfield Road. He was a lovely boy, good at sport, winning many prizes for running, was a member of St Mary's Choir, and was an expert violin player. He had enlisted in the Hussars at the outbreak of war and then, after training, transferred to the 3rd Suffolk Regiment.[38] He was billeted in a barn, somewhere in France when he fell and was injured. After a period of convalescence he re-joined his regiment on 8th August 1916. He was killed just eight days later[39].

Ernest Farnsworth

Lady Salt had also grown extremely fond of another young man whose name appears on the War Memorial - Harry Yewberry. Young Harry had endured a sad life until he came

---

[38] *Ernest is buried in Dive Copse British Cemetery, Sailly-le-Sec. In June 1916, before the Somme offensive, the ground north of the cemetery was chosen for a concentration of field ambulances, which became the XIV Corps Main Dressing Station. Dive Copse was a small wood close by, under the Bray-Corbie road, named after the officer commanding this station. Plots I and II were filled with burials from these medical units between July and September 1916.*

[39] *Staffordshire Advertiser, 28th August 1915*

to live in Walton on the Hill. He had been born out of wedlock in High Ercall, Shropshire in 1895. His mother had very little time for him and his younger brother, and their elderly grandparents brought up the two boys. By 1904 the grandparents could neither afford to care for them nor were they physically able to cope with them. Their mother had since married and had four younger children by her husband. She had no wish to take on another two hungry boys and so it was either the workhouse or be taken into the care of the Waifs & Strays Society.

Standon Farm Home

Harry was sent to St Michael's Home for Boys, Pelsall, and then, in 1907, at the age of twelve, he was transferred to the Standon Farm Home for Boys in Staffordshire. As a purpose-built farm, the Home was equipped to train boys in agricultural skills. They cultivated over 50 acres of land, which were leased from Thomas Salt MP, the late husband of Lady Salt. The boys were responsible for looking after several horses which were used to pull the ploughs and harvesters across the fields. The horses also powered the pumps that drew water from the farm's well, which was more than 150 feet deep. Most of their produce was sold at local markets, and a regular stall was kept in nearby Stoke-on-Trent. As well as their fruit and vegetables, the Home also sold butter and milk from their herd of cows. The quality of their produce was highly regarded, and they had won a special award for growing the 'Best Crops in the District'.

Boys on Standon Farm

Harry had grown into a personable young man and when he left Standon Farm Home in May, 1912, he entered into service with Lady Salt in Walton-on-the-Hill, working as a trainee footman. His wages were £10 per year, with an allowance of 2s 6d per month for washing He had been taught his new duties by John Beech who had been with the Salt family since the aged of twelve, first as a footman and now as Butler. For perhaps the first time in his young life Harry felt settled in his new home in a lovely rural village, but it was not to last. In less than five years he would be dead.

John Beech

The news of Harry's death had reached Lady Salt just days after she had heard of the death of her son Walter. Walter had been in the Lancashire Fusiliers as a young man and, after a period as a soldier, he had moved to Gibraltar to work as a Horse-Breeder. At the outbreak of War he returned to England and rejoined his old regiment as Captain. He was killed as he briefed his relief on 24th October 1916[40].

Thank goodness her eldest son and heir, Thomas Anderdon Salt had been spared. After Oxford and Sandhurst he had joined the 11th Hussars and survived a spell fighting on the West Coast of Africa and on the North-West Frontier from 1887 to 1897. He served throughout the Great War and now he was safely at home with his wife and family.

Lady Salt's Coach-man cum Handyman, Arthur Weatherer, had also seen his son, Eric, go off to war in 1916 as a strong healthy lad of eighteen. He was discharged as "no longer physically fit" after being gassed, but at least he had returned, and now he was making plans to marry his sweetheart Edith Caulfield.

Eric Weatherer

---

[40] *The Thiepval Memorial, the Memorial to the Missing of the Somme, bears the names of more than 72,000 officers and men of the United Kingdom and South African forces who died in the Somme sector before 20 March 1918 and have no known grave. Over 90% of those commemorated died between July and November 1916.*

Following the death of Sir Thomas Salt in 1904, the family home at Weeping Cross[41] had been sold to Morton Philips, Chairman of a manufacturing company making tapes and ribbons. By 1915 Morton was obliged to return to his family estates in North Staffordshire but he kept in touch with Lady Salt and other residents of the Parish. There was sadness once again when news of the death of Mark Hibbert Philips was received in October 1917. The family had continued many of the traditions of the Salt family, supporting local organisations and, providing a tea party with fun and games each year for the school children.

Morton wrote in his diary on 11th October, 1917, "I got home at 2.30. Kate is crushed but trying to bear up bravely.

We are spared the awful suspense that many have to bear, and we hope and trust that death was instantaneous."

Although Mr & Mrs Philips did not attend the dedication service they sent a generous donation towards the construction of the War Memorial.

Mark Hibbert Philips

---

[41] *Since 1915 the house has been known as Baswich House*

Dowager Lady Salt

Throughout the War Dowager Lady Salt had allowed her home in Walton on the Hill to be used for many fund raising events. She was always hospitable and the Reverend Cappell and his wife were regular visitors. Mrs Cappell and her son were staying with Lady Salt when news of the death of her husband was received. James Cappell had been a great sportsman, playing football, rugby, cricket, hockey and he also enjoyed a day's shooting. He was a fit man, so it was a surprise to find he had died, not on the battle field, but in hospital, from dysentery. He had been wounded in the summer of 1917 by a bullet in his left shoulder whilst helping a doctor attend the wounded at the Front but after a period of convalescence and a short holiday back in England he soon returned to France.

The Salt family played a major part in the life of the Parish for many years and it was a very sad day when Dowager Lady Salt left Walton to live in Chelsea. Her home was always open to visitors and it is unlikely that anyone who appealed to her for help would be turned away. There were many happy gatherings in her home, especially at Christmas time and everyone felt that her leaving the area broke a link with the past history of the parish.

Chapter 9
Nurse Lyons

Charlotte Causer stood between her twin sister Martha and her very new husband, Robert Causer, as the crowd around the memorial grew bigger by the second. They had been married just a few days, and most of those present would always refer to her as Nurse Lyons. Having relinquished her post as Village Nurse on her marriage, as all nurses were expected to do, she was grateful for the gift of over £20 which she had recently received from her appreciative patients.

She had been married just ten years when her first husband, William Lyons, died. Now, at the age of forty-six, she was to start afresh with a man whom she had known since childhood, living in the community in which she had spent most of her life. She was so looking forward to the future and it seemed as if her life had come full circle.

The daughter of railway worker Francis Smith and his wife Elizabeth, she had been born in Brocton in 1874. After leaving school she had gone to Congleton, in Cheshire, to become kitchen maid for Alfred Meakin, earthenware manufacturer. It was while in Cheshire that she met William Lyons, a travelling boot salesman, and they were married in Baswich Church in 1895. They made their home in Chorlton, South Manchester, but William died in June 1905 aged just 40, leaving her with an nine year old son, William Francis, known to all as Frank.

Before long, she was back in Brocton working as the District Nurse. It was in January, 1903 that the "ladies" of the parish first discussed the possibility of employing a nurse. It was decided to seek the opinion of parishioners as to whether they were prepared to pay a regular subscription towards the nurse's salary and their own subsequent care

Eventually the "Berkswich & Tixall Nursing Association" was established and then, by 1907, the various local nursing groups joined forces to form the "Staffordshire County Nursing Association". The first nurse, in Berkswich was Mrs Elizabeth Smith, Charlotte's mother, who was appointed in 1903 and retained the post until her death in 1907.

Following her mother's death, Charlotte was keen to better herself, and so sponsored by the Staffordshire Association, she started training at the Midwifery and District Nursing Training School in Plaistow, London. In July 1908, after completing her training, she became the Nurse and certified Midwife for Berkswich. She was required to undertake work in the area for at least three years, or else she would have to refund some of the costs of her training. Her starting salary was 15/- per week, rising to 18/- in her third year. She was provided with one new uniform each year, together with a bicycle if required! Covering Walton, Milford, Brocton and Tixall, with occasional visits to Acton Trussell and Bednall, Charlotte certainly required the bicycle! If she remained in post for four years, she would receive a bonus of £5 on the completion of her fourth year.

Staffordshire County Nurses circa 1914
Reproduced courtesy of Staffordshire Record Office.

The Staffordshire County Nursing Association set out the duties of the Village Nurse as follows: "The services of the Nurse shall be for nursing the sick poor in their own homes, without distinction of creed. Patients may be attended who, though unable to incur the expense of a private nurse, are able to make some contribution to the funds of the Association, provided that the full performance of their primary duties of nursing the sick poor leaves the nurse time for such work. Patients should be encouraged to give a donation to the Association, however small."

Regular visits to the school were a major part of Charlotte's work. Every three months she would check the heads of all the children for "nits," and often she would return to make inspections of "special cases" – children who were suffering from malnutrition, or where there was genuine concern about their care at home. Should the home not be as clean as it should be, it was her duty to induce, and teach tactfully, simple rules of hygiene and cleanliness. Regular follow up visits were often required to prevent things "slipping back". During her time as school nurse it was estimated that 80% of children had defective teeth, 50% suffered from vermin or other parasitic conditions, 20% had defective vision, and 10% were retarded by anaemia, general debility or deafness.[42] There was always something for her to do!

The safe delivery of babies was also a task entrusted to the Parish Nurse. By 1915 Acton Trussell, Bednall, and Teddesley contributed £10 per annum in return for her services in maternity cases. At one point, just before the outbreak of war, Charlotte had applied for, been appointed, and accepted a post as Health Visitor. However, after a great deal of thought she decided to remain as nurse in the area she knew so well. She was rewarded with an increase in her salary.[43] In 1915 she

---

[42] *D421 Staffordshire Record Office.*
[43] *Berkswich Parish Magazine July 1915.*

delivered thirty-eight babies, dealt with twenty-two medical and sixteen surgical cases, and made a total of 1,497 visits.[44]

Meanwhile, her son, young Frank, had gone into service, as Hall Boy in the home of Edward Samson, Vicar of Armitage near Rugeley. As soon as war broke out, Frank volunteered and was enlisted into the Royal Engineers. He was slightly wounded in 1916 but soon returned to his regiment. However, on the 21st February, 1917, he was again admitted to hospital with severe gunshot wounds to his chest. He had no chance of recovery, dying later that day.

Frank had been awarded the Military Medal, and Charlotte remembered with pride, the ceremony held during a service for soldiers on the Chase, during which she was presented with his medal. His Lieutenant wrote to her saying, "My first sight of him was on the Somme under heavy shelling when he was outside the trench, dressing the wounds of a sapper who had been hit. We hope that if any one of us has to go under we may end as finely and gamely as your son."

Often she would call in at Sister Dora Convalescent Home for a chat with the Matron, Eleanor Mills Saunders. Eleanor had been appointed early in 1917, coming from St Anne's School at Abbott's Bromley. Perhaps she could see that nursing grown men would be easier that dealing with adolescent girls!

The Convalescent Home at Milford had opened in 1884. "Sister Dora", Dorothy Wyndlow Pattison, had worked tirelessly for the people of Walsall, treating smallpox and industrial accidents which were common in the town. She had always believed that, after a serious illness, a period of convalescence was necessary. In 1887, money was raised to provide such a home and, for several years until 1898, it was run successfully by Matron Margaret Lonsdale, a long-time admirer of Sister

---

[44] D540 1–3 Annual Report Staffordshire Nursing Association, Staffordshire Record Office.

Dora. Then the money began to run out and, in 1904, a Committee of Management was established to run the home.

The new committee compiled a strict set of rules for the men and boys who would come, usually for a stay of around twenty days, from the industrial conurbation of the West Midlands. Open from the middle of March to half way through December, the home ran smoothly until the outbreak of war. Things were now about to change.

By February, 1915, the number of casualties arriving back in the UK from the Front was rising, and the committee decided to offer accommodation to a limited number of convalescent soldiers through the auspices of the British Red Cross, once the home opened its doors again in March.

Sister Dora Convalescent Home 1914

The Red Cross were delighted to accept the offer, and the Committee Chairman, Tom Byron Adams, an Iron Founder from Wolverhampton, was given the power to decide how many soldiers they could accept at any one time.

At the same meeting, the Committee had to deal with correspondence from the Military Authorities. The first request was to allow the construction of the Military Railway through the Hospital Grounds. Although they were not happy with this intrusion, permission was eventually given for the railway to go ahead, but the War Office was to pay three guineas per annum for the privilege of using of the land.

The second request from the Military Authorities was even more drastic than the first. They requested that the Committee should sell the entire hospital to the War Office as the nucleus of the Military Hospital to serve the Camp. The Committee replied in no uncertain terms that they were not disposed to sell the hospital.[45]

The Committee was comprised of several wealthy businessmen from the area including William Morton Philips who had lived at Weeping Cross, (manufacturer of braids & ribbons), William Peach, (boot and shoe manufacturer), and several directors of iron and steel companies. Sir Thomas Anderdon Salt, now a Lt. Colonel, Captain Levett from Milford Hall, Frederick Langley, a solicitor from Wolverhampton, Norval B. Graham, Proprietor of the "Express and Star" and William Harper, Assistant Secretary at Wolverhampton General Hospital completed the organising group. They kept a tight hold on things and, when Mrs Ethel Sant-Wright asked permission to use part of the home for a Coffee House for soldiers, they politely declined.

This did not deter Mrs Sant-Wright, and before long a Coffee House was opened immediately opposite the Sister Dora Home. Mrs Sant-Wright was married to Lawson Sant-Wright, a Church of England clergyman, who, in 1904, had been appointed Organising Secretary of the Church of England Temperance Society. The Coffee House Hut was funded by the Church of England and provided a rest room for those who

---

[45] *NHS-MSC 1-3 Wolverhampton Archives.*

did not wish to socialise in the Public Houses. Concerts were arranged on a regular basis when local ladies, including Cynthia Allsopp from Walton Bury and young Evelyn Bruton, daughter of the Vicar of Great Haywood, would sing as well as helping to serve light refreshments. A short service was held in the hut early on Christmas Day 1917, after which Mrs Levett presented those attending with a small pendant cross. On Boxing Day, the Vicars of Berkswich and Haywood joined forces to sing at a concert, whilst Private Crookes and Sapper Wright played on the accordion and mouth organ respectively. On each of these days those attending received a gift of cigarettes.

Across the road at Sister Dora's, the committee continued to clash with the Military Authorities. In the autumn of 1917, they agreed that they would continue to take discharged, injured soldiers once they opened again in the spring. However, they pointed out that the payment suggested by the Ministry of Pensions was totally inadequate. They also made it clear that the home would close for winter on 8th December.

However, once again the Military Authorities asked the Committee if they were willing to hand over the hospital for the exclusive use of disabled men and, if so, how soon would it be convenient to do so. The committee eventually decided that they were prepared, under the circumstances, to hand over the building until 14th March, 1918, for a rental of £25 for the period. The Authorities must pay all expenses of upkeep, together with the salaries of staff retained during the winter.

The building was to be handed back to the Committee in a condition equal to that at the time of taking over, and an inventory was to be made by Evans & Evans at the expense of the Military Authorities. All coal and consumables were to be taken at valuation.

The Military Authorities took over the home in December 1917, and it would appear that it remained in their control for the remainder of the War.

Charlotte looked around at the familiar faces standing in the cool November air. In the crowd she saw Thomas and Clara Gibson, of "The Besoms" at Brocton. Thomas was Manager of the Salt Works in Baswich Lane and she knew the family through her work. Their eldest daughter, Marjorie, (but always called Coline, for some reason no-one seemed to know) was the same age as her son.

Coline, and her younger sister Ruth, had been sent away to school in Blundersands near Liverpool at the ages of fifteen and thirteen respectively, when their mother, gave birth to a baby boy. The girls were taught to be accomplished young ladies learning French and cookery skills as well as the usual academic subjects.

Once the Military Hospital on the Chase was established, Coline had joined the Voluntary Aid Detachment[46] and Charlotte had seen her many times when she had been visiting the Hospital in the course of her nursing duties. The VAD's as they came to be called, provided free help to hospitals throughout the country. The volunteers were mainly well educated upper and middle class young ladies who could afford to provide free labour, and were anxious to "do their bit". However, the girls had to abide by a strict code of conduct and they were issued with a document stating "You are being sent to work for the Red Cross. You have to perform a task which will need your courage, your energy, your patience, your humility, your determination to overcome all difficulties.

Remember that the honour of the VAD organisation depends on your individual conduct. It will be your duty not only to set an example of discipline and perfect steadiness of character, but also to maintain the most courteous relations with those whom you are helping in this great struggle.

Be courteous, unselfish and kind. Remember whatever duty you undertake, you must carry it out faithfully, loyally, and to the best of your ability.

Rules and regulations are necessary in whatever formation you join. Comply with them without grumble or criticism and try

---

[46] *During four years of war 38,000 VADs worked in hospitals and served as ambulance drivers and cooks.*

to believe that there is reason at the back of them, though at the time you may not understand the necessity."[47]

Coline was anxious to do what she could for the war effort and by working at the Hospital on the Chase she was able to remain close to home. Unfortunately, she became one of those people who contracted flu and she died on 12th April, 1916. Her name is inscribed on the memorial, the only girl amidst the brave young men of her generation. Her parents were devastated at the loss of their eldest daughter, but they knew that her efforts had helped towards saving the lives of many a wounded soldier.

Nurse Lyons, now just plain Mrs Charlotte Causer, knew exactly how they felt. She still missed her only son dreadfully.

---

[47] *Written by Mrs Katharine Furse, the first Commandant of the British Red Cross VADs.*

(c) Berkswich History Society

Chapter 10
Rev. Gerald Hitchings - the Vicar,

I have been in the Parish six years now, and although I have been happy in my ministry it has been a sad time for us all. With the dedication of this memorial we must all look forward to better times.

I was installed in the Parish at Walton on 17th December, 1914, and afterwards I had the opportunity of meeting some of my new parishioners when we were invited to take tea in the Village School at the invitation of Captain Levett. Berkswich is so different to my former parish in Walsall, where I ministered to over five thousand people, most of whom worked in the leather industry. I was looking forward to enjoying the rural aspect of this parish and getting to know all of the eleven hundred souls in my new flock. Little did I know that before long there would be thousands of soldiers, increasing the population of the parish far beyond anything I could have imagined.

Baswich Church

I had not been in the Parish long when a young man by the name of William Williscroft, who had come to live in Walton, volunteered to start a Scout Troop. After an appeal in the Church Magazine, seventeen boys between the ages of ten and eighteen expressed an interest in joining. The cost of scout uniforms was beyond many of the boy's families, so we introduced a scheme whereby boys brought 6d per week. Once they had paid 2/6d towards the cost of their uniform they were allowed to wear it, as long as they had passed their "Tenderfoot" badge and agreed to complete the weekly payments. Baden-Powell, founder of the scout movement, had based the uniform of khaki shirt and shorts, scarf and wide brimmed hat on that worn by the South African Constabulary as this was considered the most practical outfit for the wilds. Drill was an important part of their training, and all scouts were expected to attend Church Parade regularly. Williscroft often took the boys off to Wales camping, as family holidays were out of the question for most during the hostilities. The troop also took part in competitions and sporting events against other local scout groups, to engender a spirit of comradeship.

Early Scouts in Walton

Younger boys were anxious to join in the fun and in May 1917, a wolf cub pack, for boys from eight to ten was also started.

In 1915, as a departure from the normal Harvest Festival, we asked the children to bring eggs to church. Rather a risky request, young children are not the best guardians of such delicate items. However, 180 eggs arrived intact, and sixty of these were sent to the Sister Dora Hospital and the remainder to Stafford Hospital. This proved to be such a success that the egg service was repeated each year during the war. Other churches in rural areas introduced similar services. We also held a flower service at Brocton Mission Room, the flowers going to Stafford Infirmary.

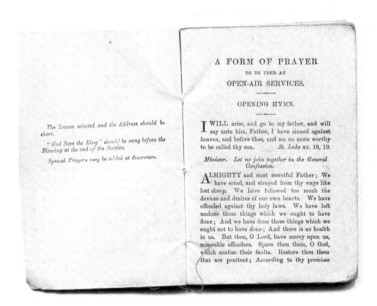

Service & Hymn Book issued to Soldiers

During the summer months we held open air services on the Chase. The form of service was set out in a book published by the Society for Promoting Christian Knowledge. Clergy were instructed to keep the lesson and address short and God Save the King was to be sung at the conclusion of the service. Such services were always well attended, as were the regular services at Walton Church. Numbers were such that it became necessary to use the organ loft and gallery at Walton, encouraging the soldiers to climb the narrow stairs. A member of the C.E.M.S.[48] was always in attendance in the gallery to make sure all behaved as they should!

William Marson

In 1915 I lost the help and support of Lay Reader, William Marson. For fourteen years he had taken morning service at the Brocton Mission but with failing health and poor hearing and eyesight he eventually found it necessary to resign. By kind invitation of Mrs Chetwynd, the choir and congregation were invited to tea at Brocton Hall and I was asked to present a fine silver salver to Mr Marson. It was engraved with the words; "Presented to Mr W.A. Marson by the Brocton Mission Room Congregation on his resignation, after taking the morning service with unfailing punctuality for 14 years. A token of affectionate regard and great appreciation, from the organist, choir and congregation who will miss him greatly and always remember his good work and many acts of kindness amongst them. October 24th 1915". Mrs Marson was not forgotten. She received a handsome leather handbag!

I suppose I first saw the real impact of the war when I took a break in Harrogate during 1915. I was suffering from gout,[49]

---

[48] *Church of England Men's Society*
[49] *Berkswich Church Magazine September 1915*

and it was suggested that the waters at Harrogate may help alleviate my symptoms.

On 16th December 1914 the Germans bombarded Hartlepool, Whitby and Scarborough. This was the first direct attack on our country and the first time for several centuries that civilians had been killed in Britain by enemy action. Whitby Abbey was damaged and Scarborough suffered greatly. Many residents, their menfolk away at the war, fled inland for safety. Harrogate became a base for many homeless people and, together with several military hospitals in the town; it was far from the genteel spa I had expected. This attack on these east coast seaside towns led to an immediate increase in the number of young men wanting to enlist - something the German hierarchy could not have foreseen.

We are justly proud of the young men from Berkswich who fought for their country but, unfortunately some soldiers let themselves and their country down. One of my parishioners, who happened to be the Mayor of Stafford at the time, Mr H.J. Bostock was approached outside his home, "The Shawms" by a young man by the name of Fred Taylor. The Shawms is a beautiful house built for Mr Bostock in 1905, in the Arts & Crafts style. No doubt Taylor could see that it belonged to a wealthy man and here was an opportunity to make a shilling or two!

Taylor had his hand bandaged; he stated he had just come out of hospital after being wounded by shrapnel in his head and hand while in Flanders. He continued by saying he had five days to spare before joining his unit again and he wanted to travel to see his wife and children in Manchester. He was entitled to some army pay but, as there was no Army Pay Office in Stafford, he did not have the train fare. Mr Bostock, aware that there had been some problems with paying soldiers regularly, took pity on him and lent him 15/- which Taylor promised to pay back as soon as he was in funds again, giving his name and number to the Mayor.

Recruiting Poster issued after the Scarborough Bombings

The Shawms

After several months and no repayment, Mr Bostock wrote to both Taylor and his Commanding Officer. Taylor, a Private in the RAMC,[50] was charged with obtaining money by false pretences. He had not been in the war and had damaged his hand unloading green groceries! Neither had he been to see his wife and children, but used the money for a trip to Leicester. He had a wife, Ethel, who he had married in June 1915, but there were no children! He pleaded guilty and asked for eight other offences to be taken into consideration. He was sentenced to three months hard labour. I supposed it saved him from fighting in France![51]

Another young soldier, Private William Furness of the Manchester Regiment, also let himself down. A fire was reported at Roadside Farm, Brocton Crossroads. A hay rick was burning fiercely and by the time the fire brigade arrived the

---

[50] *Royal Army Medical Corps.*
[51] *Fred died on 9th February, 1918 and is buried in Gorton (Manchester) Cemetery*

hay valued at £10, was completely destroyed. The following day Furness owned up to starting the fire. He appeared in Court the following week and, after an adjournment, he was handed over to the Military Authorities to be dealt with. Was this yet another attempt to delay a trip to France, or just a stupid prank?[52]

As a clergyman I was very much aware of the number of young men who could not face another spell in France. They would often go absent without leave and, when eventually caught and returned to Camp, they would choose to end their lives, either by the bullet, of which there were plenty, or by hanging, rather than go back to the battlefield.

It is sad to record the death of a soldier, not by his own hand or by the ravages of war, but by an unfortunate accident. On Saturday, 29 January, 1916, soldiers had gathered at Brocton Cross Roads to catch the 5.30 p.m. bus into Stafford. They were a rowdy crowd who had already spent some time in the Chetwynd Arms. The bus arrived - already carrying several passengers. There was a rush for the door and about 45 hefty men tried to board. James Henderson Purdie, a native of Edinburgh, was last in the queue. He was rather the worse for drink and the driver asked him to get off the bus. Three times James tried to embark, and each time the driver asked him to leave. In desperation, the driver moved off and James made a grab for the handrail in a frantic attempt to board the bus. He slipped and fell, the vehicle running over his arm and shoulder. Immediately the bus stopped and James was rushed to Stafford Infirmary where his arm was amputated. He died the following day. At the inquest into his death, his sister caused quite a stir when she revealed that James was in fact fifty and not thirty-eight, the age he had given to the army authorities when enlisting![53] Despite the circumstances of his death he was buried with full military honours in Stafford Cemetery.

---

[52] *Staffordshire Advertiser, 1st July 1916*
[53] *Staffordshire Advertiser, 8th February 1916*

Then, in August 1916, I attended the Inquest at the Barley Mow, Milford, into the death of Private Heaton Whitaker aged 19. Private Whitaker had been badly wounded in both legs and one arm, and he was in Staffordshire convalescing from his injuries. It was a beautiful, hot summer's day and a group of soldiers decided to take a swim in the River Sow at Milford. Whitaker, who was an excellent swimmer, was first to jump into the water, shouting to the others to hurry up and join him. And that was the last that was seen of him. Private Len Slater jumped in to try and find his friend but immediately he was engulfed by weeds. He was pulled to safety. The soldiers then requested the assistance of a passing boat. Whitaker was soon found, standing upright, under the water, his legs and arms encased in a tangle of weeds. He was dead. Perhaps if he hadn't suffered injuries to his legs and arm he would have had the strength to escape from the weeds but it was not to be. The Coroner recorded a verdict of accidental death.[54]

The "Glee Club" James Cappell is centre, front row

[54] *Staffordshire Advertiser, 13th August 1916*

Many parishioners talked fondly of a former curate, the Rev. James L. Cappell - a true Scot - who came to us from Old St Paul's Church in Edinburgh. News of his death came in January 1918. He had been a leading light in the "Glee Club," entertaining members of the Parish from time to time, especially when there was a need for finance for the Church.

He was curate from 1904 until 1910 when he moved to a Parish in Blackburn where he met his wife. He was married in the Spring 1914 and within a year the couple were blessed with a baby boy, Alistair. On 26th November, 1915, James became a temporary Chaplain in the Army and was sent out to France His second child, Honor was born in September 1918 but she would never know her father as he died aged just 41, before she was born. He was buried in Ste Marie Cemetery, Le Havre.[55]

To mark the fourth anniversary of the outbreak of war on Saturday, 4th August, 1918, services were held in Walton Church in both the morning and evening. The Scout Troop took an active part in the evening service, parading with the draped colours and leading the prayers. The following day an open-air service was held on the Chase at Milford. Drum Major John Guy brought a military band along and, as well as playing for the hymns, they entertained the visitors on the Chase with a programme of light music. Afternoon Tea was then served in the C.E.T.S.[56] hut.

The hut had been a great asset to the soldiers. Opened on 3rd April 1917, it provided an alcohol free zone for those who did not drink. Run by a voluntary committee of local ladies, it

---

[55] *During the First World War, Le Havre was one of the ports at which the British Expeditionary Force disembarked in August 1914. Except for a short interval during the German advance in 1914, it remained No.1 Base throughout the war and by the end of May 1917, it contained three general and two stationary hospitals, and four convalescent depots.*
[56] *Church of England Temperance Society*

provided refreshments, entertainment and somewhere to just sit quietly and write a letter home.

A billiard table had kindly been donated by the Vicar of Bradley, a piano was on loan from Mrs Wilmot-Sitwell,[57] and the committee had raised funds to buy a gramophone.

One of the happiest occasions I can remember is the marriage of Harry Hooley of Bank Farm, Brocton to Ida Whitehouse, who lived on Radford Bank. Harry was the first

demobbed soldier to be married at Berkswich, and it was an especially joyous occasion as Harry had been a prisoner of war for nine months. Of course I had married many other soldiers during the war, but often it was rather a rush job after a young lady had been led astray by a handsome fellow in uniform from the Camps on the Chase.

Although hostilities ended in November 1918, the damage done by the war lingered on. My younger brother Frank, received his commission in May 1915 and managed to survive all the fighting. However, he met his death when a shell exploded while he was carrying out salvage work at

---

[57] Mrs Wilmot-Sitwell was related by marriage to the Levett family of Milford Hall.

Auberchicourt, France on 3rd December 1918, just three weeks before his 40th birthday which fell on Christmas Day. Frank wrote "Apepi and Nefertari: A Tragedy in Two Parts" a story in verse which has recently been published posthumously. Perhaps, if he had lived he may have been a great poet or writer.

Although he is unknown to the Parish, I have been deeply moved by the letters I have received from so many local people and to find that his name has been added to those on the Roll of Honour is very emotional.

Another friend, Major Harold Leggett, died in March this year[58] as a result of injuries he received fighting in France. Major Leggett was one of the first officers to come to Brocton Camp in 1915. He lived temporarily in Walton and then in Milford before going to France to fight. He was a regular churchgoer and often read the lesson during Evensong at Walton Church. Before the outbreak of war, Harold was a school teacher in Nottingham but he knew Stafford well as his uncle had been Governor of Stafford Gaol, an occupation that must run in the family. His father was for a number of years Governor of Worcester Gaol.

Maud Earl lived on Radford Bank and she waited throughout the war for the return of her sweetheart, Roland Deaville, son of a Stowe by Chartley farmer, but whom she had met when he was working as a draughtsman at Siemens factory. He had been boarding at the Trumpet Inn just a few doors away from her home. The couple were married at the first opportunity when Roland returned home in September 1918. However, he was not in good health being seriously wounded whilst fighting in France. He died of pneumonia in February 1919 after just four months of marriage and was buried in Stowe by Chartley Churchyard. They had been so looking forward to a future together.

---

[58] *1920*

(c) Berkswich History Society

In February 1917 I conducted the burial service of a young soldier by the name of William Richard Bradford who now lies in our church yard. It is a sad story. The Bradford family had lived in the tiny village of Woolhope, Herefordshire for several generations but in 1912 Joseph, the eldest son of Richard and Ruth Bradford, appeared in Court and was found guilty of indecent assault on a thirteen year old girl from the village.[59] The family were ostracized, so they left the area giving no indication as to where they could be found. They came to Brocton, where their family history was unknown. Joseph enlisted in the army in 1915 and then on 22nd January, 1917 young William, aged 18, attended the Recruiting Office in Lichfield where his medical classification as to fitness for service was C1. This indicated that he was fit for Garrison Service at Home Camps and free from serious organic disease. He gave his address as The Green, Brocton and his father, Richard, as his next of kin. On 2nd February he was sent to Bradford, in Yorkshire, to start his training. By 24th February he was dead. He had been admitted to the Bradford War Hospital where he died of acute pneumonia. Were the conditions so intolerable that William contracted pneumonia within days of arriving in Bradford, or was the Medical Officer who examined him in Lichfield so keen to enlist recruits that he failed to notice that the lad was already ill? Whatever the reason, he was buried with full military honours, his body being conveyed to the Church on a gun carriage. A service of remembrance was held for him at Brocton Mission Church. Shortly after this, the family left Brocton and attempts to find his father to return William's personal possessions to the family failed despite extensive enquires being made in Staffordshire and by the Police in Herefordshire and Gloucestershire. The Bradford's had once again disappeared from the face of the earth.

Two other soldiers, who died during the early months of the war, are buried in our church yard, far away from their homes and families. They are Frank Sellars, just twenty from

---

[59] *Hereford Times 9th November 1912*

Lincolnshire and a much older man by the name of Arthur Bennett, aged forty-four who died in December 1915.

However, it has not all been sadness. We enjoyed our Peace Festivities immensely. Saturday July 19th, 1919 was observed as a national holiday of thanksgiving for peace. About two hundred children from the parish were entertained to tea in the school, and then marched down to Milford Hall where Captain Levett provided swings, pony rides and trips in a rowing boat on the lake. Numerous presents had been hidden on a small island in the lake and at intervals various groups of children could be seen searching for the hidden packets. Once the children had departed for Milford Hall tea was served in the school to all the widows in the parish and then those who wished could join the celebrations at the Hall. Races had just begun when the rain started, which put an end to all the fun. It was agreed that the sports would be held in the evening of 28th July, weather permitting, to be followed by a fireworks display.

A celebration for the whole parish had been planned for 7th August, 1919, but this had to be postponed on account of the bakers strike! The bakers were striking for a wage of £4 per week, a 44 hour working week, and the abolition of night working.[60] Not all the bakers were on strike, but bread was strictly rationed to a 2lb loaf for every 3 people in the household and, to get a loaf, it was necessary to join the long queue at the Market Hall.

Eventually the strike was settled and the celebrations took place on Wednesday afternoon, 13th August in the beautiful grounds of Milford Hall. Four large marquees, two bell tents, tables and seating accommodation were lent by the military authorities, and the band of the Lancashire Fusiliers was in attendance. They provided light music during the afternoon and, in the evening played for dancing. A pig competition

---

[60] *The Bakers settled for a basic wage of £3 for a 48 hour week. A rise of five shillings.*

caused great amusement. To catch the creature blindfolded was impossible, and numerous men and women tried to do what seemed to be hopeless. Afterwards, the pig was turned out into a field and was eventually caught - the prize, the pig. The ladies of the Parish catered for over 500 people. Tea was served to everyone, beer provided for the men, and demobbed soldiers received cigarettes.[61]

During the past twelve months we have seen great changes in the Parish. The Twigg's whose family have been continuously recorded in the Parish Registers since 1609 have left the area. Lady Salt has gone to London to live and Brocton Hall Estate has been sold by the Chetwynd family. Then in February, Captain Allsopp of Walton Bury and one of the founders of Walton Cricket Club died. We have lost several stalwarts of the community, who have supported us both financially and spiritually. Now we must look to the future and hope and pray that, never again do we see such slaughter between nations.

.

---

[61] *Berkswich Parish Magazine.*

Chapter 11
We made it Home

Among the many people surrounding the Memorial there was a scattering of military uniforms. These were the young men who had made it home and were now looking forward to a normal life – whatever normal means after experiencing the horrors of war. One young man in naval uniform was Frank Brown who, on leaving school, had become a locomotive fitter

Frank Brown and best friend Charlie Attwood

for W.G. Bagnall Ltd, world renowned manufacturer of steam engines, especially for narrow gauge railways. His brother William was also employed as a fitter, whilst their father worked in the company's foundry. When war broke out Frank decided to make use of his industrial experience and he joined the Navy as an engineer. Much of his time during the war had been spent on H.M.S. Thrasher, a destroyer, patrolling the North Sea around the Orkneys, Shetland and into Scapa Flow.

Frank had been involved in the dramatic capture and eventual sinking of a German submarine on 8th February, 1917. The British Merchant Ship "Hanna Larsen" was on her way to Tyneside when, about 20 miles from Spurn Point she was fired on by the German submarine UC-39. She attempted to flee, full steam ahead, but eventually the master, realising that they could not outrun the submarine, ordered the crew to abandon ship and take to the life boats. Within minutes the submarine went along-side the life boats and took the Master, Thomas Read, and the Chief Engineer, Scott, prisoner. The "Hanna Larsen" was looted and then sunk by the UC-39. The remaining crew were just abandoned in the life boats.

The following morning UC-39 was at it again, this time shelling the "Ida" in Bridlington Bay. Then H.M.S. Thrasher appeared on the scene.

H.M.S. Thrasher

"Thrasher" did not hesitate, but shelled the U-boat which attempted to crash dive. Water poured into her engine and control rooms, and the German crew began to panic. The Commander decided to surrender and gave the order to surface. The Thrasher opened fire again just as Commander Oberleutnant Ehrentraut emerged from the conning tower. He was killed. The U-boat was still making speed on the surface, and the destroyer continued to fire. Three of the German crew jumped into the sea and were drowned, while three others on the deck were killed and several were wounded. Finally the submarine was hailed by megaphone and ordered to stop. This she did, and the remaining members of the crew were taken prisoner. Mr Read and Mr Scott of the "Hanna Larsen" were found in the ward room, none the worse for their adventure.

There was an attempt to tow the sub into harbour but it was taking on water and eventually sank before reaching port.

It was only the second voyage of the UC-39, one of the most modern vessels in the German fleet. However, the Engineer on board the submarine was not a lucky omen. He had been on eight German vessels including a battleship, cruisers, motor launches and now a submarine, all of which had been destroyed!

Frank remembered that day vividly. Although it was a great triumph to destroy a submarine that had caused so much havoc in the North Sea, his abiding memory was of the young German sailor who shortly after being rescued and brought on board the "Thrasher" as a prisoner, died in his arms.[62]

Shortly afterwards the Captain of the Thrasher, Lieutenant Ernest Hawkins received the following letter

Dear Sir,

I am taking this opportunity of writing to you to thank you and your shipmates for the very kind way you treated Mr Scott, my Chief Engineer, and myself the day you rescued us from the German submarine.

The Germans gave us the choice of death, whether we preferred to be hung or shot. You gave us no choice at all, but only tried to kill us with kindness and if ever it lays in my power to return the compliment I will not be backward in doing so. I am sorry to say one of my Crew died in Grimsby hospital and two of the others are still detained there.

I have got everything square now, and am leaving Tyneside dock today as Captain of the S.S. Primo of Newcastle bound for Rouen in France and I only wish I could meet you

---

[62] *This young man is now buried in the German Cemetery on Cannock Chase.*

and your shipmates there. I can assure you we would paint the town red.

I suppose you had been thinking by now that I had forgotten all about your kindness to us, but no fear. I have had a good deal of extra work to do owing to losing my ship, but if you are ashore in the Tyne when you come home and have time to call at the above address, I have left orders that you are to be treated to the best of everything and the password is to be "Thrasher". So with best wishes to you and all your shipmates,

I remain,
Yours truly,

T. Read, Late Master of S.S. Hanna Larsen.

****

The Woods Family home in Walton on the Hill

Brothers Bill (Walter William) and George (George Samuel) Woods were at the memorial, together with their parents, Samuel and Katherine, and their sister Rita. They had both survived the war – just! Everyone knew the Woods boys as they lived in the thatched Post Office right in the centre of Walton, next door to the forge where Mr Thomas Fletcher had been the blacksmith for so many years. Before the war Bill had helped his father with his plumbing and painting business, and George had been a postman. His mother was the village postmistress.

On the 8th of September 1914 the brothers had gone along to the Borough Hall to enlist into the Grenadier Guards. They were sent immediately to Caterham Barracks, the home of the Guards, for training. After completing basic training, an appeal went out for anyone who knew anything about flying! As the Wright Brothers had made their maiden flight of twelve seconds in December 1903, it was unlikely that anyone knew very much!

Walter William (Bill) Woods

George (3rd from right, front row) and his Unit

However, the authorities were keen to find mechanics to service the aeroplanes which were used initially for photographic reconnaissance. Bill and George both volunteered, but only Bill went to France. In April 1917 he was promoted from Corporal to Flight Sergeant. George served with the Royal Flying Corps in England as he was not as physically fit as his brother.

Bill had a very narrow escape from death when a plane burst into flames after crashing into the hanger in which he was working. He was very badly burned and returned to the UK from France to convalesce close to home, at Sandon Hall Military Hospital. Chief Mechanic 4686 Woods was demobbed on 26th February 1919, Medical Category B II.

In 1908 Charles Crooks gardener, arrived, from Droitwich to work for the Allsop family at Walton Bury. He came with his wife and two daughters, Edith and Annie. The girls were just a little younger than the Woods boys, and there was certainly an attraction between them all. However, Mrs Crooks did not like life in Walton and after two years in the village, the family returned to Worcestershire. The two girls regularly revisited the village to see the Woods household and especially their friend Rita. These visits ceased in 1914 when travel became more difficult and, in June 1917, Edith married John Willmore, a teacher who, at the outbreak of war, had joined the Worcestershire Regiment as a Second Lieutenant. John was killed in France on 5th November, 1917 after less than six months of marriage - very little of which was spent with his new wife.

Once the war was over, Bill would regularly cycle over to Droitwich to visit the Crooks girls. There was romance in the air![63]

George had married Amy Smith in September 1917. He met Amy when he had been stationed at the Royal Flying Corps training aerodrome, Harlaxton, just south of Grantham. Now they were back in Stafford and he had plans for their future! All the huts on Cannock Chase were being sold off during the early months of 1920 and George had been able to buy two of them.

George & Amy in 1919

---

[63] *Bill and Edith were married at Walton in June 1924.*

He planned to erect them on the main Lichfield Road in Walton, where he hoped to be able to establish a garage business in one of them. He was sure cars would be the future. They were to live in part of the other hut, and Amy, who had learnt about the butchery trade from her family, would make and sell pies and sausages from a small shop. The future looked rosy for George and Amy!

Amy's father outside his shop

***

Joseph Alfred Orchard was only fourteen when war broke out and was too young to go and fight, but he was soon in uniform, working in the Army Pay Corps. With so many men joining the army, the Pay Corps had to engage 11,000 specially enlisted Clerks and 15,000 civilian Clerks to cope with all the extra work.

Joseph was born in Wales but, when his father died in 1903 leaving his wife with four young children including a four year old and a toddler, the family came to Stoke on Trent, his mother's home town. She needed help and support from her family.

Young Joseph Alfred Orchard

After leaving school Joseph joined the Army Pay Corps and somehow, in the course of his duties, he managed to injure his shoulder and neck. As a serving soldier, be it only on the home front, he was sent to the Military Hospital on Cannock Chase for treatment and to recover. His smart military uniform was replaced by a shapeless grey-blue outfit which did nothing to impress the girls. It did, however, indicate to everyone that he was a wounded soldier doing his bit for King and country and not a conscientious objector!

Joseph and his friend Frank Trewin

Perhaps his injury had been a blessing in disguise, as it was while on the Chase that Joseph met a young lady by the name of Winifred Edwards who lived in Brocton. She must have been able to see past his rather shapeless uniform, and the couple began to "walk out" together.

After recovering from his injuries, Joseph returned to work in Derby but before long had the opportunity to volunteer to return to Stafford and work at the Camp on the Chase. Now he would be able to see Winifred once again!

Winifred Edwards

The couple were married in Derby in June 1920 and were now amongst the crowd surrounding the memorial. They looked so young - Winifred was eighteen and Joseph was not quite twenty-one. He had been demobbed from the army, had no job, and they were living with Winifred's parents in a small cottage in Old Acre Lane, Brocton. What would the future hold for them?[64]

What would the future hold for everyone?

---

[64] *The Orchard family remained in Stafford and Winifred lived to be over 100.*

Part II
France & Belgium 1919

In Flanders fields the poppies blow
Between the crosses, row on row,
That mark our place; and in the sky
The larks, still bravely singing, fly
Scarce heard amid the guns below.

We are the Dead. Short days ago
We lived, felt dawn, saw sunset glow,
Loved and were loved, and now we lie
In Flanders fields.

Take up our quarrel with the foe:
To you from failing hands we throw
The torch; be yours to hold it high.
If ye break faith with us who die
We shall not sleep, though poppies grow
In Flanders fields.

John McCrae
1872 – 1918

In September 1919, just ten months after the end of the Great War, Maud Sophia Levett left her home, Milford Hall, near Stafford to travel with her daughter Dyonèse and her son's batman, William Farndon, to find the grave of her son Richard, killed in 1917, and that of her nephew Jacinth Wilmot-Sitwell, killed in July 1916. This is her story. With the exception of the photograph of Madame Zoe, and the cartoon of "Old Bill", all the pictures were taken on that journey.

A Mother's Journey to France & Belgium, 1919

Having decided to go to France the first thing was to get our passports which was a matter of time, and, though I applied on September. 2nd for the renewal of mine obtained from the passport office in 1916, I was still without it the week of our departure. Fearing that our plans might altogether be upset in consequence, I went to London on September 24th to enquire at Coutts Bank, where it was supposed to be waiting for me. I found nothing was known of it there, and I had to go to Lake Buildings to make further enquiries where I found myself in a very mixed and excited crowd of all nationalities. One woman, of eastern origin, was having a loud voiced quarrel with a stolid policeman who finally edged her to the door and told her to go outside and stay there.

I was then shown the way to Cook's department where a nice clerk told me the Passport had been sent to the central office at Ludgate Circus. There were piles of passports on the table which were being tossed over by a very ragged little scout, and one ceased to wonder at any confusion or delay. After that, to Ludgate Circus where, at last, I obtained possession of the precious document. I then set out to look for a room but, after trying my club and six hotels and a Lodging House in Ebury Street, I felt quite incapable of any further effort and threw myself on the mercy of 31 Chester Square[65] where I found a most kindly welcome.

The next morning I started for the French Consulate where I had arranged to meet Dyonèse and Farndon, to get our passport visa. I was told I had to produce another photograph and two references in France before I could get through. As I had neither photographs nor references I felt in despair for a moment but asked the Commissionaire to let me see someone to whom I could explain the object of my journey. I was shown upstairs where a kindly Frenchman said under the

---

[65] *The Levett family had owned 30 Chester Square when Dyonèse was born.*

circumstances references were unnecessary, but a second photograph was indispensable and told me where to go to get one taken in an hour. I then set off for Euston to meet Dyonèse and take her with me to the shop. Together we went and sat for the most hideous portraits imaginable. Mine has since been committed to the flames.

We got luncheon at Frascatis whilst waiting and then, armed with the photographs, we again went back to the French Consulate. This time we were shown into a sort of pen and told we must wait for about an hour and a half for our numbers to be called but found my number had been one of the morning's issue. We protested and were told we might go upstairs where we found another crowd waiting behind a screen which divided a large double room. After waiting patiently for some time, the temptation to see what was the other side of the screen was too great, and I lunged gently through the opening and found myself in the inner room where the passports were being signed. The Commissionaire tried to push me back, but by this time Dyonèse and Farndon had joined me, and once in, we did not mean to go out. Somehow we got a place at the table and, after the very casual young Frenchman had lit his pipe half a dozen times and set alight to the wastepaper basket with his matches, he eventually looked us up and down, signed our passports, and out we went. We crossed the Square to the Belgian Legation where we were shown into the kitchen. There we again got our papers signed and we then set out for Charing Cross.

We just missed the 4 o'clock express. Happily the next train left in about half an hour and we arrived at Folkstone in time for dinner and, after a breath of sea air, we went thankfully to bed after a most exhausting day.

The next morning we were up in good time so that we might get on board before the crush. We were successful in getting good seats and a comfortable berth for me before the

Boat Express came in. This was fortunate as there was a dreadful crush and the crossing was quite exceptionally bad. The cabin was crowded with wretched people all desperately sick lying about on the floor or anywhere they could. I never felt so ill in my life! Dyonèse remained on deck but was reduced to the state of a drowned rat, having quite ceased to care that the spray was breaking over her, absolutely saturating her fur coat. At Boulogne the crush was awful. People tried to squeeze up to the gangways but their bundles and bags got caught in those of others and made a solid block. An

Maud Levett & Farndon on board ship

enormous Frenchman caused great amusement by getting stuck in the gangway and then shouting in great excitement that he had never been so insulted in his life.

A nice little Padre from the Y.M.C.A. came and carried off our passports to get them stamped for us and, at last feeling very much the worse for wear we scrambled down the gangway. Some hot coffee was very refreshing, after which we pulled ourselves together to make some plans. We had quite hoped and intended to go first to Noyelles-en-Chaussée, near Crécy to see old Madame Magnier where Dick had been billeted, but the trains proved to be quite impossible. One had left at 12, an hour before we had arrived at Boulogne and the next did not start till 6.30 a.m. which would have meant spending half a day and a night at Boulogne. Very reluctantly we had to give up this plan, and finding that a train was starting for Amiens in half an hours' time, we decided to go by that.

One saw the first signs of the war at Boulogne where the quays and railway sidings were filled up with every kind of thing – stacks of iron beds, masses of barbed wire, iron sheeting, railway engines, lorries, and every conceivable thing, all waiting no doubt for transport. There were the remains of endless railway sidings, dumps of all sorts of stores, huge supplies of hay under tarpaulins, and parties of Chinamen or German prisoners wearing the bright apple green cloaks and trousers of the French gangs, busy loading up trucks. At Etaples and Le Touquet there were still large camps to be seen. At the former place, used as a big hospital, there is a large cemetery lying beside the railway. It was not however, till we approached Amiens that we saw actual signs of destruction. In the marshy meadows, where the cattle are now grazing amongst the sedgy pools and poplar trees, one could see the pit mark of an occasional shell. The railway bridges approaching the town and the station have been shelled and a great deal of damage done in some parts of the town. When we arrived at the Hotel Belfort, to which we had been recommended to go, we found ourselves lodged in rooms which bore the recent signs of repairs to wall and ceiling, some parts of the house having been badly damaged.

Dyonèse went to see the Cathedral which is still barricaded with sand bags, the glass all being removed from the windows and consequently there was very little to be seen. I took the opportunity of a quiet time to rest.

At ten o'clock the next morning we started for Albert by train. It was whilst waiting for the train that we bought a Paris Daily Mail and first knew about the strike.[66] We took our tickets and asked where the train started from.

---

[66] *Railway transport was paralysed in the UK for nine days in September and October by a strike.*

The View from the Estaminet

No one seemed to know which platform it was and everyone gave us different information, but at last we settled down with a crowd of people who all seemed to wish to go the same way and, after waiting for almost an hour, our train came in. The trains are all of interminable length and very late. They creep along as the lines are only lately repaired so that one sees a great deal of the country. We had to change at Longueau, the next station to Amiens, where we had another long wait. At last our train arrived and, as there was a terrible crush of people, a dear old Belgian peasant and his wife came in to our carriage, making their way to Ypres. As we advanced up the line to Albert, the signs of wreckage and confusion became more apparent until we came to the town which is a hopeless mass of ruins. The Cathedral is now a mere heap of bricks and rubble, with no sign left of the statue. The streets are absolutely demolished, the houses nothing but heaps of rubbish and skeleton roofs in desolate piles on every side. We walked through the town and at once made our way to the Communal Cemetery which lies at the junction of the Meault and Fricourt Road. Farndon was very thoughtful and kind, and made us stop at a little Estaminet to get a cup of coffee on our way. He and Dick had stopped at the same place for refreshment, and we found the same woman in charge though she had left the town during the worst of the attack. The Military Cemetery adjoins the Communal Cemetery, and we found it without any difficulty. A working party had just arrived and had straightened one or two of the graves. Otherwise it was in a very forlorn and overgrown state. On two sides it is bounded by the Communal Cemetery, and on the third by rough ground where there is now a small camp in which a labour company is quartered. They are occupied in bringing in the isolated dead for burial in the cemetery. On the forth side runs the Albert-Fricourt Road.

Albert Cathedral

Across this road there is a large French Camp. We had some difficulty in finding our dear Dick's grave, as the original cross had been broken off and another smaller one put in its place. Eventually we found it, a little apart from the others, overgrown with rough grass and weeds. Someone had planted two little roots of pinks and a tiny rose bush on it. A party of "Tommies" under a nice Scotch Sergeant were at work in the cemetery and they helped us in our search for the grave. When found they set to work to clear it up, trim up the grass and level

Dick's grave

the earth round it. They also planted a small root of lavender which I had brought out with me, fetching some good earth to plant it, in and making use of the water provided for their own tea to water it. The Communal Cemetery nearby is in a terrible state; the monuments shattered, the graves broken open and the coffins and bodies thrown up by the shells and still unburied as there is no one left in the town to restore the place to order. We stayed some time at the cemetery and Dyonèse took some photographs but unfortunately the day was very dark with a leaden grey sky, and the light was very bad.

It all seemed part of the tragedy of the surroundings - something unspeakably forlorn and sad, but somehow it all combined to make one feel it did not matter. Nothing mattered and nothing was real but the all-pervading spirit of the place.

We had found Dick's grave and it was empty – quite simply he was not there. With an intensity that must be realised to be understood, one felt conscious of the eternal purpose above it all and the abiding spiritual presence to which one was linked by the tie of love.

As we left the cemetery we saw a wedding party come to lay immortelles[67] on one of the graves. We were told afterwards that the bride had only one leg, the other having been blown off by the same shell that wounded her mother and killed her sister. On returning to the town we found a little wooden shanty calling itself the "Hôtel de la Paix" and we went in to get some refreshment. It was kept by a very nice Scotchman, Fletcher by name, who we thought at first was a Frenchman as he spoke such perfect French. In reality he was Scotch but had served in both the British and French armies in the Intelligence Department. He had won the Croix de Guerre for an act of bravery which led to him being Court Marshalled by the British Officials. During his absence, his motor bicycle was shelled, and he was charged with neglect of duty in leaving it! He showed us his Cross and papers, and we made great friends with him and his wife who gave us some excellent soup and ragout for which we felt very grateful. We then set out for Aveluy, passing the piled up wrecks of houses, all one great heap of ruins. I found a coffee pot, with a bullet hole through the bottom and side, which I carried away as a souvenir of the place.

Shells of all sorts and sizes were lying about in every direction. It is dangerous to touch anything, and one cannot walk a yard from the road without risk. The day we were at Albert, a ploughman was killed tilling the ground and a soldier wounded by an exploding shell. The day before two children had been killed poking about in the ruins.

---

[67] *Everlasting flowers or a china replica of flowers used as a graveyard monument.*

Aveluy is not far from Albert, about 3 kilometres, and we set out to walk along the road by the railway line. Of course every bank and ditch or shelter of any kind is full of dugouts, and every inch of the way one saw the wreckage of the war.

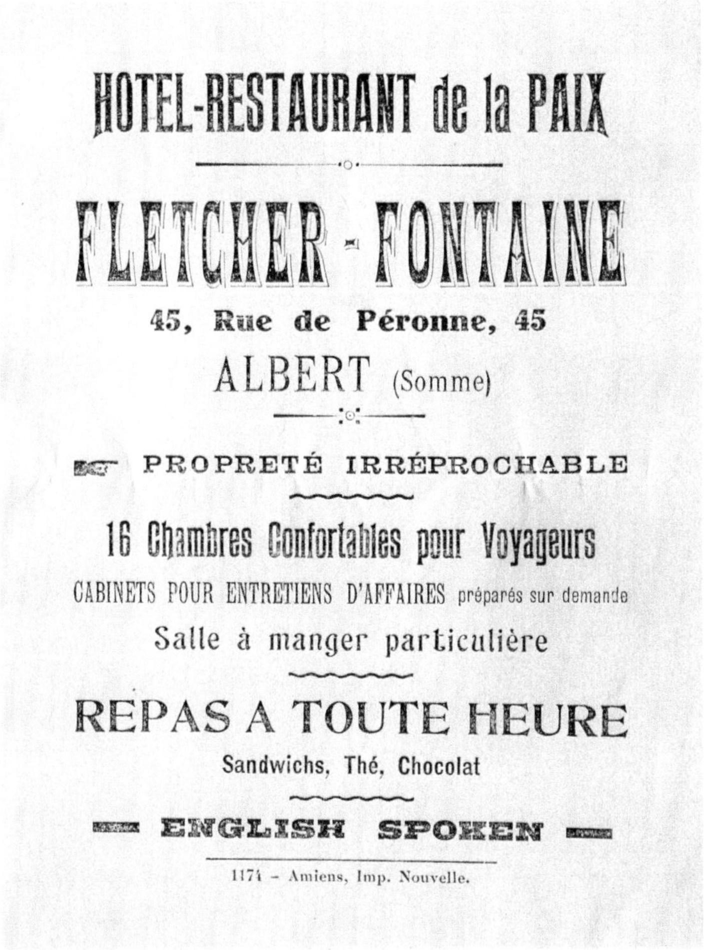

HOTEL-RESTAURANT de la PAIX

·○·

FLETCHER - FONTAINE

45, Rue de Péronne, 45

ALBERT (Somme)

:○:

PROPRETÉ IRRÉPROCHABLE

16 Chambres Confortables pour Voyageurs

CABINETS POUR ENTRETIENS D'AFFAIRES préparés sur demande

Salle à manger particulière

REPAS A TOUTE HEURE

Sandwichs, Thé, Chocolat

ENGLISH SPOKEN

1174 – Amiens, Imp. Nouvelle.

A party of engineers were repairing the line and collecting shells, which are being exploded and one hears them going off in every direction. German prisoners in their bright "frog" green cloaks and caps were also working on the road and railway. We arrived at Aveluy, but the place was hardly recognisable.

When Farndon had left it was a village, or something approaching a village, but, since the German advance and the deluge of shells which we had poured upon them in their retreat, it had been reduced to a mere heap of wreckage. Not a single building was of any recognisable shape. The house where Dick had been billeted had still one tottering wall standing but a large shell had evidently hit it fair and square and had gone through to the cellar exploding inside and blowing up the whole place into one tangled heap of ruins. We saw the wall of the room where Dick had slept, the cupboard where the provisions had been kept, and the stair case going down to the cellar where the cook had lived. Otherwise there was nothing of any sort or recognisable form. We passed the bridge over the Ancre which was being repaired by a gang of German prisoners and then crossed the causeway which had also been badly damaged. On either side of the causeway there is a sort

Dick's Billet

of morass where Dick used to skate, but the breaking up of the Causeway has let out the water and now there is nothing but a sea of mud out of which one still sees the skeleton ribs of mules and horses sticking up.

Crucifix Corner is just beyond the Causeway, but no remains of the crucifix are left except a rusty iron bar in a block of concrete. We sat down here to rest awhile, and I picked some cornflowers which were growing beside the road. One sees signs of many pretty flowering plants but most of them are now over;

only cornflowers, poppies and a few pale blue scabious remain. After a little rest we passed on "up the road" as Dick called it. "I saw Eley going up the road" he wrote. This road was the one which led through Dicks camp and went "up the line". It was a long straight road rising slowly to the crest of a ridge. On either side was a scene of unspeakable desolation. Miles and miles of churned up earth, one continuous mass of shell holes covered with rank weeds which grow to a prodigious height. Behind lies Aveluy and, in the distance, Albert. On the different ridges around one sees shattered roofs and rubbish heaps surrounded by stark grey stumps – once trees - all that remains of the surrounding hamlets. There are no trees in this part of France except round the villages or in the small marshy ravines with which the country is intersected, and often a group of these skeleton trunks is all that marks a village. Here and there, in the churned up ground, one sees a solitary cross or a little group of crosses. Shells and ammunition of all kinds lie thick upon the ground. We walked to the top of the ridge and there saw before us the great mine crater of La Boisselle[68] and the place where the village had been, but there is not the least remnant or trace of the village left. There is nothing but a succession of shell holes and, just off the road, this crater which looks like an immense chalk quarry. It is surrounded inside with

The great mine crater of La Boisselle

[68] *The largest man-made mine crater created in the First World War on the Western Front. It was laid by the British Army's 179th Tunnelling Company Royal Engineers underneath a German strongpoint*

German dugouts, but the path round the crater is so narrow and slimy that it is somewhat risky going on it

A fall to the bottom would leave little but broken bones. Here we turned back as it was getting late and we set our faces towards Albert coming down the Pozières road, along which dear Dick's last journey was made. There were endless groups of little crosses by the way, and working parties are camped along the road for bringing in the isolated dead and clearing away the debris. The "tommies" all seemed so pleased to see English faces. The poor peasants at Albert are so marvellously brave and one sees old men trying to till their little plots of ground at the risk of their lives, and the women with wheel barrows collecting bricks and trying, bit by bit, to make some semblance of a home. One family were sitting in a room with only three walls to it, having a meal. Everywhere the French people are shrouded in black and they look unspeakably sad. One party arrived by train, probably for the first time to see their home, in floods of tears.

We made our way to the station after having had some tea with our friends at the "Hôtel de la Paix" who gave us their own little room, as the wedding party had been having a feast and filled the public room with fumes of smoke and food. Madame came and talked to us during tea and told us how not an inch of the land had been uncultivated before the war. Now it is just a wilderness, as much iron as earth, and it is impossible to imagine how it can ever be tilled again. She said that the children had become so unmanageable and a perfect scourge since the war, as they had lost all sense of fear having been so much with the soldiers and having no one but women in the home. They had run wild, and the whole generation of them seem to be sadly misled.

Another long wait for a belated train and then we arrived back at Amiens in time for a late dinner.

On Sunday morning we started by the same train for Poperinge via Arras, Douai and Hazebrouck. We again had a long wait and a change at Longueau. By the time we arrived at this place it was raining. We were travelling only light and had no umbrellas and, as there was no glass in any of the station roofs in these parts, we just sat on our baggage on the platform in the rain. Amongst the crowd waiting for the train, we had noticed a very charming looking French woman with a very refined sad face shrouded in crépe and carrying a large bunch of flowers. She saw me sitting in the rain and came and stood near me, offering to shelter me with her umbrella. We then began a conversation and I found that she was on the way to Albert where her mother had lived, and where her husband was buried, and that she was just going to the cemetery to take flowers to his grave. I told her about dear Dick and, with tears in her eyes, she told me that she would make his grave her care and that she would go to it that very day and put some of her flowers upon it. She had lost her husband and her son-in-law during one year of the war. She gave us her address and we hope to keep in touch with her. We parted company at Laugeau and got in the train for Arras on route for Lille, and there began a truly wonderful journey right across the most famous battle fields. The train travelled very slowly as the line was still under repair in many places. The railway embank-ment was full of dug outs, and one seemed to see "Old Bill" and his jam and bully beef tins at every yard. We passed Aveluy again, running under the bois d'Aveluy, or rather past the shattered stumps which are all that remains of the wood, with the Ancre, a tiny river, on our right.

Old Bill

We could also see the Grévillers ridge and Lourpart Wood, a clump of tree stumps on the right. The village of Irles was a little distance from the line and on every side we saw the same shattered ruins with stark grey tree trunks round about the remains of little hamlets and villages. The river had made a channel for itself as it winds through the country which is marked by a sort or ravine in some places very narrow, in others widening to 70 or 100 yards wide. There is a steep bank which has been wooded with trees on either side of the ravine and in the bottom is a sort of quagmire filled with reeds, tall bullrushes and rank grass. In some places there are pools, in others only bog but the whole ground has been torn and mangled and pitted with shell holes. The trees which have been blasted with gas are mere stumps. We passed Mesnil and Beaumont Hamel and endless other wrecked villages as we travelled up the line, in fact we passed over the ground where much of the worst fighting took place. It was a sight which defies all powers of description. As dear Dick said, "the abomination of desolation", and mile after mile as the train crept slowly across the country one saw nothing but the indescribable waste, the burial ground of countless "Unknown British Soldiers" who must have perished in the mud and water- logged shell holes.

We passed Arras and then on to Douai across ground which has been less devastated as it was more or less behind the line, but Douai is in a miserably shattered state and the street fighting there and the fights for the great slag heaps, or "Fosses" as they are called, has made it memorable.

We reached Lille in time to get some luncheon and then started again for Hazebrouck at 2.30 p.m. passing once more over the devastated area of Armentières. It was so extraordinarily interesting having Farndon with us as he had been over the ground practically all the way, having marched from Paris into Armentièrs, and then on to the Ypres Salient, then back again to the Somme and he recognised each road and village as we passed. As we approached Hazebrouck we saw Mount Kemmel in the distance which has quite changed its natural shape having been soiled and wooded on the top. Now it is flattened, the south having been torn away by the ceaseless shelling. Having some time to wait at Hazebrouck we found a café where a very charming French woman provided us with a most excellent tea, real butter and plum jam and after tea we walked about the little town waiting for our train. We tried to go to the Church but the old curé told us it was locked up and the services were all over. We took a photograph of a beautiful old 17th century building on three sides of the square, now used as French cavalry barracks but alas it has not come out and as there seemed nothing else to do we sat in the rain on a bench in the square "looking at life" till it was time to start again. It was a strange and very wonderful Sunday.

Our train to Poperinge was very late and as we crept along the darkness fell. At the frontier a Belgian Official opened the carriage door, poked in his lamp, looked round and left us in peace. No one asked to see our passports. A little Scotch officer travelled in the carriage with us, returning to his billet at "Skindles", the name given to what was an officer's club at Poperinge started by Neville Talbot, the Bishop of Winchester's son, during the war, but now an hotel run under the same name by a woman and her daughter who took it over from Mr Talbot and were there through much of the fighting. Hazebrouck and Poperinge were places where the troops rested when out of the line. We also were making for "Skindles" so the little Scotchman attached himself to us and kindly helped to carry our kit.

On arrival we fortunately had an excellent dinner of soup, bottled asparagus, roast beef and lobster salad. During dinner, some officers who came in gave us a concert. One man played the piano extremely well and the little Scotch officer fancied himself very much on the violin. They played all the latest jazz and waltzes, and eventually got the waiter to move the tables with a view to dancing - quite obviously in the hope that Dyonèse would be a possible partner, but Madame intervened and suppressed them. Somehow one felt it was all part of the life of the place. Under other conditions it would have jarred terribly but it just seemed to be a bit of the past. It was just what the boys had been doing all those awful years – coming out of the line to rest – living it up with various entertainments for a brief spell – then going back, perhaps never to return. One could imagine them in the Club room still decorated with amazing types of feminine beauty frescoed on the walls, and one felt the place was full of ghosts. And these men were just the same – "Carrying on".

Madame Zoe of "Skindles"

Suddenly the pianist broke into the beautiful hymn "Love Divine all Love Excelling "which, strangely enough, I had last heard sung by the boys in the Chapel at Eton, little thinking when next I should hear it. Then he jazzed up and made it into a dance tune. I shall never forget that dinner or the concert which lasted till late in the evening. We were feeling overstrung and tired, and everything seemed ridiculous and we laughed at nothing, but as Farndon so truly said, out there one must either laugh or cry and, that evening. we were in a strange borderland between the two.

"Skindles"

Monday morning brought the most glorious sun. We were up early and started for Ypres before ten o'clock, stopping on our way to get a photograph of a most delightful team of dogs. On our arrival we walked down the line to the Reservoir Cemetery where I wanted to look for Eustace Bourke's[69] grave. We found the cemetery quite easily as Farndon knew the spot well, having last passed it running for dear life as it was being shelled by the Bosch. We found two rows of graves marked "A" but, in both, the 6th cross was missing. It was impossible to

---

[69] *Son of the 8th Earl of Mayo killed on 16th June 1915*

identify the grave but, no doubt, it was one or other of the two without a name. The cemetery was well kept and planted with annuals. The method of keeping the graves is to have them in long plots joined together, turfed over and raised about a foot from the level of the ground. There is a strip of soil left all along the top of the plot in which annuals have been sown and some plants planted and in this strip of soil the crosses are set. The crosses on the officers graves' are of various sorts and kinds having originally no doubt been put up by the different regiments but where they have been broken they are updated by the plain little crosses that mark the graves of the men. Each one has a stamped metal label with the name and regiment on it. So many are put up to "An unknown British Soldier". In most cases the cemeteries are in very good order. Many are bright with flowers, and one generally sees "Tommies" at work amongst the graves. The sergeant at the cemetery at Albert told us that the Labour Battalion was responsible for putting them tidy, and they will then be handed over to the Graves Commissioners.

Belgium Dog Team

We then went through the town till we came to the turning to Boesinge and took that road, passing the Canal Lock on our right and turning sharply to our right at "Suicide Corner". The name was changed to "Salvation Corner" by some staff officer who thought the former name depressing for the men! We walked along the paved road in the most glorious sunshine, finding our thick clothes very hot.

Gun emplacements Salvation Corner

We went on to Essex Farm cemetery. We had some difficulty in finding dear Jacinth's grave as a small shrub had been planted on it which had grown so large it hid the name on the cross. In the direction in which the graves face, there is .a most beautiful view of the ruins of Ypres with the Cloth Hall and St Martin's Church framed with a clump of poplars on one side, and low bushes on the other. It all looked very peaceful the day we were there, and from the cemetery there is no view of the wreckage of the battle fields. We stayed for some time, putting a cross of blue scabious on Jacinth's grave, and then turned our steps back towards Ypres along the road littered on either side with remains of all sorts. The tracery of the Cloth Hall still shows in some places, and the shattered fragments of St Martin's Church close by make altogether a picture of exquisite beauty and pathos. Albert strikes me as the wreck of a world of happy peasant homes, but Ypres seems in some way to be inspired and full of the most tragic beauty.

After lunch we walked through the town, past the Templars Hall and out by the Lille Gate. Every house in Ypres is the remains of a fortress, the rooms barricaded with sandbags and iron sheeting, and every cellar was a dugout. One wonders, as one passes, how many lives have perished beneath the wreckage.

Ypres

The Belgians seem to take much more precautions about the danger from explosives, and have notices up everywhere warning people of the danger of disturbing the ruins. At Albert no one cares where one goes or what one does! We passed St Peter's Church which is a mere shell, but on the north wall outside there remains an immense Crucifix about 30 feet high which is practically untouched, except for a shrapnel wound to the neck.

We passed on across the railway towards Zillebeke where again the village is a mere heap of ruins, the Church only recognisable as being a larger pile of stones and rubble than any other. The grave yard has, to some extent, been levelled and some of the graves restored to order and marked with broken relics of the tomb stones. Some of the vaults are still open and you can see the poor bones and smashed coffins, and in one place a body, quite unrecognisable, wrapped in the fragments of its grave clothes torn out of it leaden coffin which is standing outside of the vault. At this place the peasants are building quite useful little huts of wood on concrete foundations and tilling little plots of ground, in an attempt to return to some kind of normal life.

On Tuesday morning we started for Ostend, and we again passed through the extreme left of the Salient. This I think was the most tortured bit of ground we passed over and we found all the remains of the front line fortifications, miles of barbed wire, sand bagged dugouts, broken trenches, the wholesale wreckage of trains, burnt out trucks, engines buried upside down in the mud, crumpled rails, every imaginable sort of refuse and everywhere and always the endless shell holes filed with stagnant green water, mud and debris. How any human being could ever have lived in such conditions is beyond belief and to attempt any true description is impossible. One simply feels it is all too big for words and one understands like never before, the silence of those who have lived through it.

At Torhout we had to change trains and wait some time. We got some lunch at a café the proprietor of which had been the unwilling host of a German Staff Unit for four years and a day. They took possession of his house and made him pay them rent, only letting him have a corner of his place to live in and they never paid one sou for anything they had.

We spent the night at Ostend and had the privilege of paying £2 for our dinner, soup, sole and buttered eggs for 3!!! The sole cost 27 francs!

Some 500 civilians were killed at Ostend principally by our big naval shells. The railway station is quite knocked to pieces and the harbour partially blocked with a sunken destroyer but these things seemed to make but little impression on one's mind after all that one had seen.

Ypres

There is not one spot in the Ypres Salient I think where from one point of view or another, one does not see a cemetery with its regiment of crosses recording the resting places of the thousands and thousands of those who fought and died and whose bodies were found and received Christian burial and reminding one of the great company of the heroic dead whose graves are unmarked by any cross and whose remains are part of that awful waste of upturned earth or who lie in the countless bogs and shell holes where the water, weeds and rough herbage and wild flowers are gradually making them a shroud of nature's weaving.

Appendix

Letters from the Front

Many letters came to Staffordshire from the Front, usually sending messages of affection to parents, wives or children. They gave nothing away regarding where they were, or what they were up to. The Censor saw to that!

However, this letter from Billy Walker, one of a collection of letters sent to his parents, describes vividly the bombardment of the German troops. We believe he is fighting somewhere near Rouen, as in an earlier letter he writes about meeting Frank Twigg, who was at Repton School with him. We know Frank was stationed at Rouen.

"I think we've really "got em beat" now and it's only a question of time. Our artillery is terrific and munitions plentiful now! But it is to be hoped that Munitions Workers will not relax their efforts. One cannot realise the quantity of shells fired until one has seen and heard our "Barrage". In a real bombardment the sky is lit up at night like the worst of thunderstorms magnified a thousand fold – perpetual flashes of lightening. The noise is like constant thunder, not the distinct explosion of each gun, but an undulating roar, going on the whole time, with every few seconds the tremendous crash and boom of the "Heavy Guns" close at hand and the shriek of the shell as it hurtles away into the distance. Firing to a programme, starting altogether, almost to the second, they cease so suddenly; leaving the night still, save for the regular firing which continues day and night without a break. "

Postcards

Often there was not time to write long letters so a postcard often said all that was to be said. The following cards were sent from Rugeley Camp.

THE SOLDIER
TO HIS WIFE.

I'VE said it before, I say it again,
 I write it down now with paper and pen,
There are Wives and Wives for the married men,
    But there's no Wife like mine!

My comrades in khaki their homes all miss,
The comfort, the rest, the fireside, the kiss,
Yet who of them knows my memory's bliss,
    There's no Home like mine!

I see it all now as in cinema show,
It makes life worth living with friend or with foe,
Is there anything better? I answer back "No!"
    There's no Wife like mine!

If thus of Wife and Home I make my boast,
Although apart we drink yet one more Toast,—
"Of lands we love the land we love the most!"
    There's no Land like mine!

And so I raise to-night to God my prayer
For Wife and Home and England fair,
To God Who gave them me my praise I bear,—
    There's none like mine!   C.F.P.

RUGELEY CAMP

* * *

THERE'S an isolated, desolated spot I'd like to mention,
    Where all you hear is "Stand at Ease," "Slope Arms,"
    "Quick March," "Attention."
It's miles away from anywhere, by Gad, it is a rum 'un,
A chap lived there for fifty years and never saw a woman.

There are lots of little huts, all dotted here and there,
For those who have to live inside, I've offered many a prayer.
Inside the huts there's RATS as big as any nanny goat,
Last night a soldier saw one trying on his overcoat.

It's sludge upto the eyebrows, you get it in your ears,
But into it you've got to go, without a sign of fear,
And when you've had a bath of sludge, you just set to and
    groom
And get cleaned up for next Parade, or else, it's "Orderly
    Room."

Week in, week out, from morn till night, with full Pack and a
    Rifle,
Like Jack and Jill, you climb the hills, of course that's just a
    trifle.
"Slope Arms," "Fix Bayonets," then "Present," they fairly put
    you through it,
And as you stagger to your Hut, the Sergeant shouts "Jump
    to it."

With tunics, boots and puttees off, you quickly get the habit,
You gallop up and down the hills just like a blooming rabbit.
"Heads backward bend," "Arms upward stretch," "Heels raise,"
    then "Ranks change places,"
And later on they make you put your kneecaps where your
    face is.

Now when this War is over and we've captured Kaiser Billy
To shoot him would be merciful and absolutely silly,
Just send him down to Rugeley there among the Rats and
    Clay
And I'll bet he won't be long before he droops and fades
    away.

* * *

BUT WE'RE NOT DOWNHEARTED YET !

Other cards were sent from the UK to the Front to show the patriotic feelings of those at home.

London is watching :-"All's Well!"

Great Britain & Ireland.   France.   Russia.

Belgium.   Servia.   Japan.

THE·FLAGS·OF·ALLIES·AND·FRIENDS · WHO
FIGHT · IN · FREEDOMS·CAUSE.

Back came cards showing the devastation that had been inflicted on France.

40 — La Grande Guerre 1914-18 — ALBERT en Ruines — La Rue de Boulan   L.T.

24 — La Grande Guerre 1914-18 — ALBERT en Ruines   L. T.
Rue d'Amiens   Amiens Street

Names on Berkswich War Memorial

CAPPELL James Leitch*
COATES Robert*
DEAVILLE Roland*
FARNSWORTH Ernest*
FELTON Harry   (From Stafford but worked at Hazelstrine Quarries before the war)
GIBSON Marjorie*
GREEN Alan Frederick*
HARDING Levi Farrington   (Believed to be related to Miss Birks of Brook House, Milford)
HARVIE Edward Alexander Gordon*
HOLLOWAY John Thomas   (From the Lock House, Baswich. Had spent 4 Christmas's in France. Originally reported missing but died in hospital)

HUGHES Lionel Holford
LEIGHTON Harry   (Lived in Milford with his married sister)
LEVETT Richard William Byrd*
LYONS William Francis*
MARSHALL Thomas   (Lived at Radford and worked as a Farmer's Boy)

McFERRAN Maurice Anderdon*
MELLOR James William   (Lived at Acton Hill)
MORT Paul John*
ROGERS Ralph   (Believed to be son of John & Mary Rogers of Weeping Cross)

SALT Walter Petit*
SMALLWOOD George*
TILSTONE Leonard*
TRUNDLEY James*
TWIGG Francis William*
WIGGIN Harry   (Uncle of Ethel & Thirza Wiggin, maids for Richard Hand)

WILTON Richard Birkinhead*
YEWBERRY Harry*

Additional Names in Walton Church
CLAYTON Francis
KIDWELL Osmund *
LEGGETT Harold *
WILMOT-SITWELL Jacinth *

* Mentioned in the text.

(c) Berkswich History Society

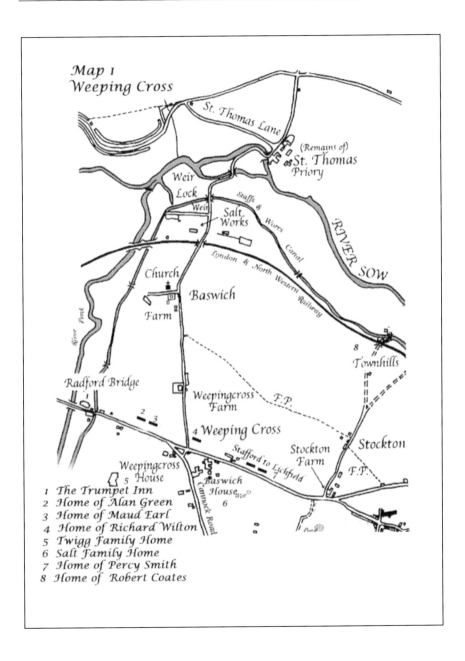

Map 1
Weeping Cross

1 The Trumpet Inn
2 Home of Alan Green
3 Home of Maud Earl
4 Home of Richard Wilton
5 Twigg Family Home
6 Salt Family Home
7 Home of Percy Smith
8 Home of Robert Coates

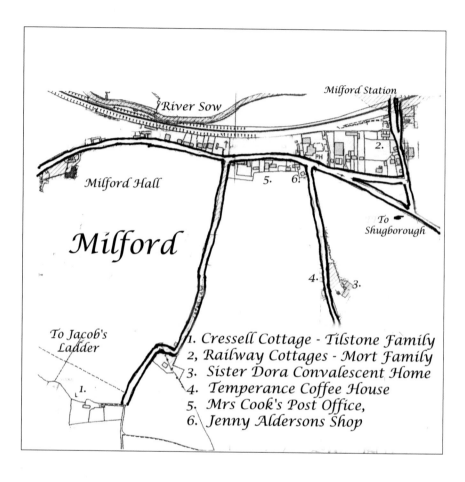

Map 2 - Milford

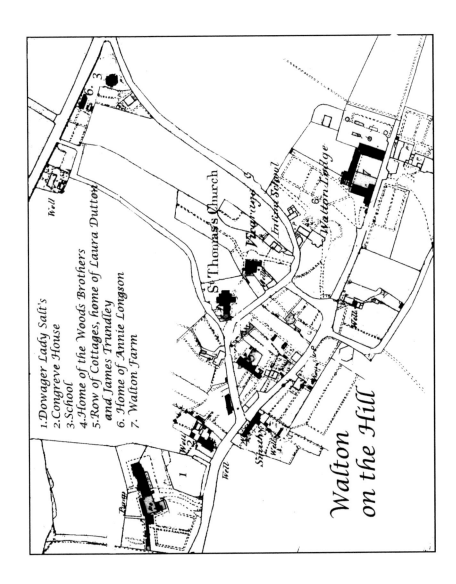

Map 3 – Walton on the Hill

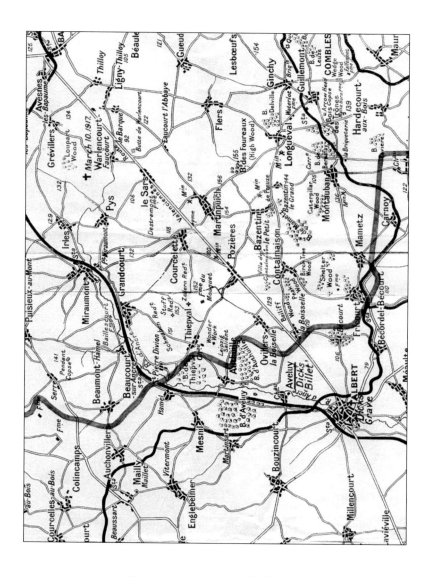

Map 4 – Area around Albert

Facts

Berkswich Women's War Association was formed in November 1915 and closed in March 1919. During that time 2,220 articles of clothing were completed.

By the beginning of 1915 over 1 million men had volunteered.

Army guidelines stated it should take 450 men 6 hours to build a 275-yard front-line trench system.

Trenches were often 3 feet deep in water.

Gumboots were provided but they were often punctured by barbed wire

On 19th July, 1916 the British Army lost 60,000 men on the first day of the Battle of the Somme.

The ground was often a quagmire and it could take six men to carry one stretcher.

By the end of the war 80,000 men were diagnosed as having suffered shell-shock.

An estimated 8 million horses died during the war.

Currency in 1920

Farthing		one quarter of a penny
Halfpenny		half of a penny, 480 in a pound
Penny	1d	twelve to a shilling
Shilling	1/-	twenty to the pound, now 5p
Florin	2/-	two shilling piece, now 10p
Halfcrown	2/6	two shillings & six pence,
One Pound	£1	a bank note equalling 240 pence.

In 1914 the average wage for a basic 58 hours working week was 16 shillings and 9 pence. By 1918 the working week was 52 hours and the average weekly wage was 1 pound 10 shillings and 6 pence.

Around 60% of the family budget went on food in 1914. Nowadays this has fallen to only 12%.

Bibliography

The Three Decker Parish Magazine
The Story of Berkswich Retold   Berkswich History Society
A Town for Four Winters,   C.J. & G.P. Whitehouse
They Pulled our House Down   Berkswich History Society
Stands the Church Clock   Dyonese Rosamond Haszard
Before the Houses Came   Marjorie Knight
Down by Jacob's Ladder   Laura Husselbee
Letters of an English Boy   Richard Byrd Levett
Down Memory Lane   Compiled by Jim Foley
Life in the Trenches   Robert Hamilton.
Stafford Remembered   S.C.C. Local History Dept.
Great War Camps on Cannock Chase   C.J. Whitehouse & G.P.
                                     Ibbotson.

Census Returns 1841 – 1911
Berkswich School Log Book
Staffordshire Advertiser.
Stafford Newsletter
Lichfield Mercury
Hereford Times

Acknowledgements

Richard Haszard of Milford Hall and Richard Haszard, Senior, for information and use of family documents.

Anthony Groucott for the use of "Lucky Black Cat" card

Church of England Children's Society for information relating to Harry Yewberry.

Dr Andrea Tanner Archivist of Fortum & Mason.

Jim Foley for permission to use information and photographs collected while he was Youth & Community Officer at Walton High School especially those of the Dutton family.

Jean Wooster for permission to use her father's memoirs

The staff of the William Salt Library, Staffordshire Record Office, Wolverhampton Archives and Stafford Library for their help and assistance.

Thanks also to the following local residents and members of Berkswich History Society who have assisted in various ways in the production of this book :-

Jean Alden, Ben Alcock, Gill Bentley, Brenda Cardwell, Nadia Davies,   John & Michelle Haddon, Anne Harper, Ian Hazelhurst, Dorothy Keeling, Alf Millar, Joan Moore, Robert Morton, Jim Smallwood, Christopher Phillips, Harvey Woods

Index of Names